SpringerBriefs present concise summaries of cutting-edge research and practical applications across a wide spectrum of fields. Featuring compact volumes of 50 to 125 pages, the series covers a range of content from professional to academic. Typical topics might include:

- A timely report of state-of-the art analytical techniques
- A bridge between new research results, as published in journal articles, and a contextual literature review
- A snapshot of a hot or emerging topic
- An in-depth case study or clinical example
- A presentation of core concepts that students must understand in order to make independent contributions

SpringerBriefs in Statistics showcase emerging theory, empirical research, and practical application in Statistics from a global author community.

SpringerBriefs are characterized by fast, global electronic dissemination, standard publishing contracts, standardized manuscript preparation and formatting guidelines, and expedited production schedules.

More information about this series at http://www.springer.com/series/8921

Timina Liu · Shuangzhe Liu · Lei Shi

Time Series Analysis Using SAS Enterprise Guide

 Springer

Timina Liu
Canberra, Australia

Shuangzhe Liu
Canberra, Australia

Lei Shi
Kunming, China

ISSN 2191-544X   ISSN 2191-5458 (electronic)
SpringerBriefs in Statistics
ISBN 978-981-15-0320-7   ISBN 978-981-15-0321-4 (eBook)
https://doi.org/10.1007/978-981-15-0321-4

This Springer imprint is published by the registered company Springer Nature Singapore Pte Ltd.
The registered company address is: 152 Beach Road, #21-01/04 Gateway East, Singapore 189721,
Singapore

Preface

This book is devoted to time series and panel data analysis, modelling and fore-casting using SAS EG. It covers basic concepts and methods for data analytics and statistical modelling, with a practical focus which utilises functions of the "Time Series" task in SAS EG.

We hope this book is a helpful guide for university students, applied researchers, professionals and those who are interested in using SAS EG to analyse their time series and panel data.

We would like to gratefully acknowledge the Australian Bureau of Statistics, Cengage, Pearson, SAS Institute and Wiley for their permission for us to use the data sets, illustrative examples and other materials including screen shots of the SAS® product.

We would also like to acknowledge the support from Shanghai Lixin University of Accounting and Finance, the University of Canberra and Yunnan University of Finance and Economics.

We would like to thank P. Dewick for reading an early version of the manuscript.

This book would not have been possible without the unwavering support of our families and friends.

Canberra, Australia   Timina Liu
Canberra, Australia   Shuangzhe Liu
Kunming, China   Lei Shi

Contents

Chapter 1
Introduction

Abstract Time series analysis is widely utilised in many areas, from business fore-casting to the prediction of population sizes of species. Various types of time series models and techniques are studied, ranging from analysis and inference to classification and forecasting. It is important to determine the appropriateness and accuracy of these models and techniques before applying them. This book is devoted to time series data analysis using SAS® Enterprise Guide® (SAS EG). The base SAS® program is widely used at universities, research institutions, government departments, and business sectors in many different areas, both public and private. SAS EG is a point-and-click, menu-driven data analysis software which is driven by the power of SAS. In this first chapter, we will briefly cover:

- The purpose of this book
- The basics of time series data
- An introduction to SAS EG

Keywords Autocorrelation · Data frequency · SAS® · SAS® Enterprise Guide® · SAS® Enterprise Guide® project · SASHELP library · Time series

1.1 Purpose

To our knowledge, there is little literature discussing time series analysis utilising SAS EG. In this book, we intend to fill this gap and focus on how SAS EG (version 7.13) can be used to analyse time series data. This book will cover some theory behind time series analysis with a largely practical focus. For further details on the

---

Electronic supplementary material The online version of this chapter (https://doi.org/10.1007/978-981-15-0321-4_1) contains supplementary material, which is available to authorized users.

development of time series, methods and applications in various areas, see e.g. Box and Jenkins (1976), Diggle (1990), Liu (2004), Kakamu and Wago (2008), Shumway and Stoffer (2011), Greene (2012), Liu et al. (2014, 2015, 2017), Zhu et al. (2015, 2016), Wooldridge (2016), and Hyndman and Athanasopoulos (2018). For basic ideas and practical techniques with SAS examples and/or the VARMAX procedure in SAS, see e.g. Ajmani (2009), Milhøj (2013, 2016) and Brocklebank et al. (2018).

1.2 Significance of Time Series

Wooldridge (2016) defines a time series data set as a series of observations on one or more variables over time. Time is an important dimension in a time series data set because past events can often influence future events in the context of social sciences and other areas. Various fields such as economics, finance, management, education, health, biology, chemistry, physics and engineering extensively analyse time series data. Some examples of time series data include:

– Automobile sales figures
– Stock prices
– Annual crime rates
– Rates of infection
– Temperature figures

Two key features of time series data are the data frequency and the presence of autocorrelation. Data frequency refers to the frequency at which the data is collected. Common frequencies are daily, weekly, monthly, quarterly and annually.

Autocorrelation, also known as serial correlation or lagged correlation, is the correlation between the observations of the same variable over successive time intervals. Many economic variables tend to display autocorrelation and/or trends over time, and may also exhibit a strong seasonal pattern. For example, autocorrelation may be used to see the impact of past stock prices on their future price.

1.3 Introduction to SAS EG

In this section we will provide a brief explanation of the basics of SAS EG.

The base SAS System provides a powerful framework for analytics and is widely used in a number of areas in statistics and data science, including business analytics, data analysis and predictive modelling. It has extensive data manipulation capabilities to conduct analytic and modelling tasks, as well as reporting tools for presenting results. However, learning the SAS language and programming SAS code to run the appropriate procedures may not be straight-forward for a beginner. This is where SAS EG is advantageous.

SAS EG is a Windows client application which provides the power of SAS in a user-friendly graphical user interface (GUI). It enables users to obtain outputs through a point-and-click interface by making selections from a series of menus without having to write any SAS code. Even for experienced SAS programmers, SAS EG provides a valuable framework within which to organise the data, tasks, and results involved in performing statistical analysis. In addition, code scripting is still available in the interface, providing experienced users of SAS with the flexibility to create and modify existing SAS code and new users of SAS the opportunity to read and learn the underlying SAS code.

There are a few books and SAS support sites devoted to the fundamental introduction and application of SAS EG and management of data; see e.g. Constable (2010), Slaughter and Delwiche (2017) and

- The SAS EG site, available at: https://support.sas.com/en/software/enterprise-guide-support.html
- Getting Started with SAS EG, available at: http://support.sas.com/documentation/onlinedoc/guide/tut71/en/menu.htm
- SAS/ETS® 15.1 User's Guide, available at:https://support.sas.com/documentation/onlinedoc/ets/151/etshpug.pdf

For an introduction to SAS EG used in Statistics, Davis (2007), Der and Everitt (2007) and Meyers et al. (2009) offer an extensive account of data analysis, regression modelling or survival analysis. For business analytics, Parr-Rud (2014) provides a beginner's guide with SAS EG.

1.3.1   Getting Started with SAS EG

When we open SAS EG, the Welcome window will allow us to choose between opening an existing project or starting a new project.

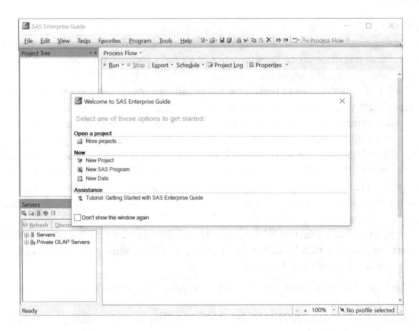

Once a new project has been opened, the default application layout contains the Project Tree, the Resources pane, and the workspace area. By default, the Resources pane is displayed in the lower-left corner of the SAS EG window, and it provides access to the Tasks pane, SAS Folders, Servers, the Prompt Manager, and Data Exploration History. By default, the Resources pane displays the Servers.

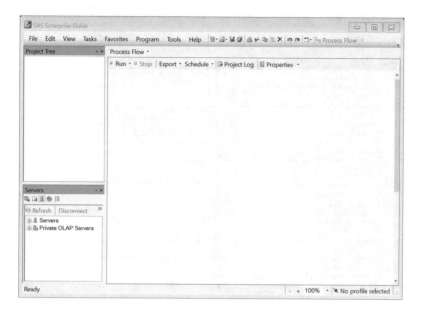

The workspace area is the main area of the SAS EG application and displays the data, code, logs, task results, and process flows. Initially, the process flow is the only window that is open in the workspace area. When we generate reports or open data, other windows open in the workspace with a tabbed interface. We can also use the recently viewed items menu in the upper-left corner of the workspace to navigate between the windows.

In SAS EG, the work that we do is saved as a 'project', which is the collection of our data, tasks, programs, and results. The project tree displays a hierarchical view of the active project and its associated data, programs, notes, and results. In SAS EG, we use tasks to do everything from manipulating data, to running specific analytical procedures, and to creating reports.

We can have one or more process flows in our project. When we create a new project, an empty **Process Flow** window opens. As we add data, run tasks, and generate output, an icon for each object is added to the process flow. The process flow displays the objects in a project, any relationships which exist between the objects, and the order in which the objects will run in the process flow.

There are several ways to get help with your work in SAS EG. Comprehensive help is available by selecting **Help** and then **SAS Enterprise Guide Help**. From this window you can browse the table of contents and index, or you can use the search feature.

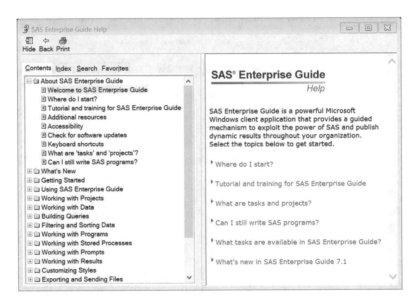

1.3.2   Data Input

Before we can create reports or run analytical procedures, we must add data to our project. We can add default SAS data files to our project, or import other types of files, including those created by other software packages such as Microsoft Excel.

Adding Default SAS Data to the Project

SAS contains over 200 data sets by default in the SASHELP library. These data sets are available to use for examples and for testing code, and some have been used as examples in this book. For information on these datasets, see: https://support.sas.com/documentation/tools/sashelpug.pdf.

When we open a data set, a shortcut to the data is automatically added to the current project in the Process Flow window and the data opens in a data grid. As an example of how a data set is displayed in SAS EG, let us consider the AIR data set which is available in the SASHELP library by default—the same as Series G in Box and Jenkins (1976). The AIR data set represents the number of passengers every month from January 1949 to December 1960. To display it, double-click **Servers** → **Local** → **Libraries** → **SASHELP**.

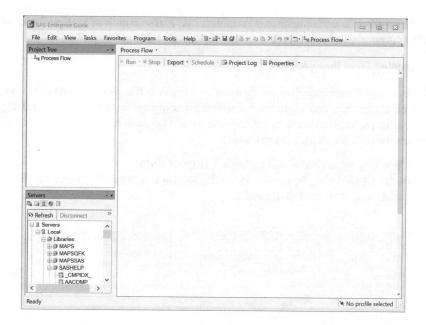

Scroll down the list of datasets to find the AIR data set and double-click it to view
the data.

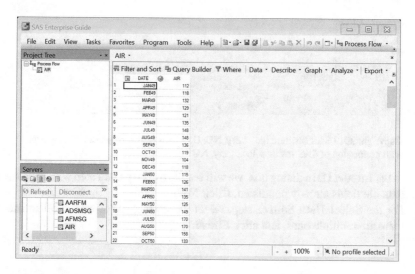

The AIR data set contains two variables: *DATE* (the month of observation) and *AIR* (the number of passengers observed for that month).

Importing Data into SAS EG

We can import data into SAS EG from an existing data file which can be in a .xlsx, .csv or .txt format. The Vegemite Price data set compiled in Berenson et al. (2013) represents the assumed cost of a 375-gram jar of Vegemite from 1995 to 2008. We import the data into SAS EG as follows:

1. Click **File** on the Menu bar, and select **Import Data**.
2. In the Open dialog box, navigate to the location of your file, select the file to import and click the **Open** button.

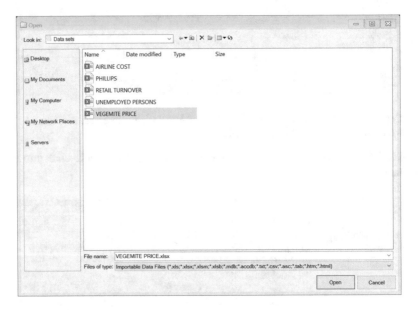

3. In the **Import Data** dialog box, we will see the **Specify Data** step with the source data file fields already populated. Click **Next**.
4. For the **Select Data Source** step, select the correct Excel worksheet to use if there are multiple ones, and click **Finish**.

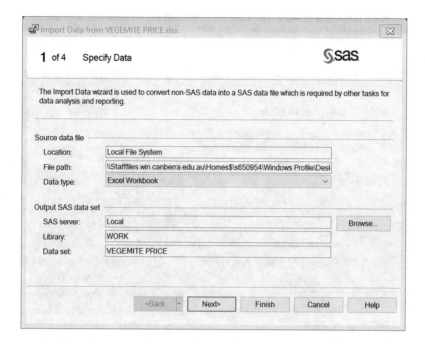

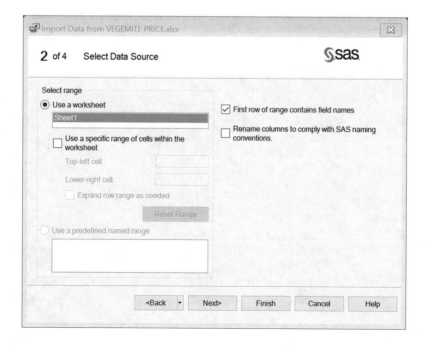

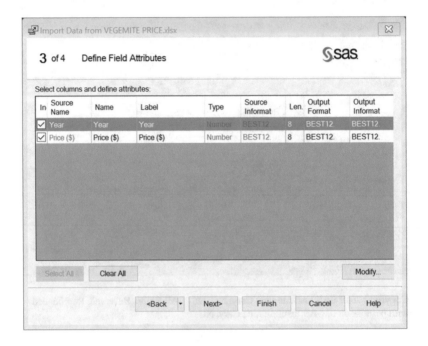

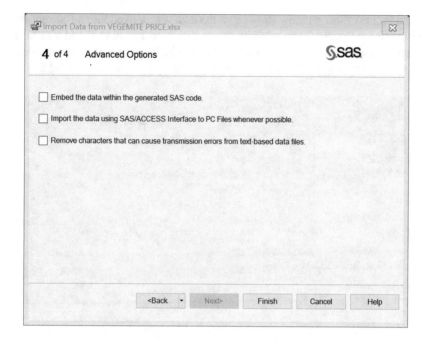

After clicking **Finish**, the data will be imported into SAS EG.

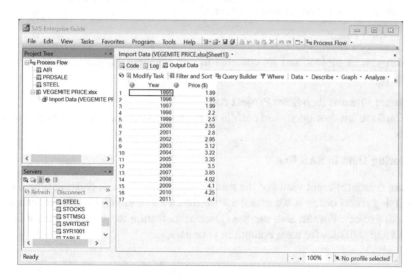

The Process Flow window shows how the data was derived into its current state. The following Process Flow window shows that AIR, PRDSALE and STEEL are default SAS data sets and that no additional manipulation was performed. We can also see that the Vegemite Pricedata was imported from a Microsoft Excel file.

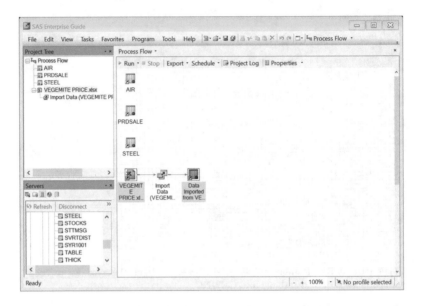

Copyright 2019 SAS Institute Inc., Cary, NC, USA. All Rights Reserved. Reproduced with permission of SAS Institute Inc., Cary, NC

Saving the Project

We can save a project and its contents to any location. Projects are saved as a single .egp file.

1. Select **File** and then **Save Project As**.
2. The Save window opens and enables us to choose the location to save the project to.

Exploring Data in SAS EG

We can create different views of the data by selecting columns, creating filters, and specifying a sort order. If we create a view that we would like to save, we can add it to our project. We can also use the Quick Stats feature to quickly generate basic graphs and statistics for each column in your data.

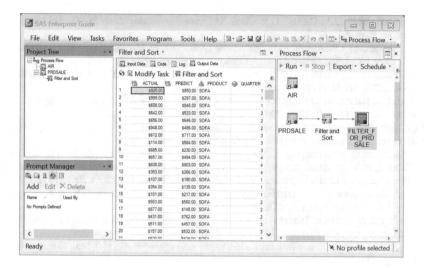

1.4   Moving Forward

For the remainder of the book, we will proceed as follows. We first lay the foundational basics in Chap. 2, and then devote each of the following four chapters to a corresponding function in the "Time Series" task in SAS EG.

In Chap. 2, we discuss basic analytics, data analysis and regression models. In Chap. 3 we cover the basic features and forecasting of time series data, followed by ARIMA modelling and forecasting in Chap. 4. We study regression analysis with autoregressive errors in Chap. 5 and finally discuss regression analysis of panel data in Chap. 6.

In the appendix, we list the data sets referenced in this book and additional relevant online examples documented by SAS. In the glossary, selected statistical terms are briefly explained.

References

V.B. Ajmani, *Applied Econometrics Using the SAS$^{®}$ System* (Wiley, Hoboken, 2009)

M.L. Berenson, D.M. Levine, T.C. Krehbiel, D.F. Stephan, M. O'Brien, N. Jayne, J. Watson, *Basic Business Statistics: Concepts and Applications*, 3rd edn. (Pearson, London, 2013)

G.E.P. Box, G.M. Jenkins, *Time Series Analysis: Forecasting and Control*, Revised edn. (Holden-Day, San Francisco, 1976)

J.C. Brocklebank, D.A. Dickey, B.S. Choi, *SAS® for Forecasting Time Series*, 3rd edn. (SAS Institute, Cary, NC, 2018)

N. Constable, *SAS® Programming for Enterprise Guide® Users*, 2nd edn. (Copyright SAS Institute Inc., Cary, NC, USA, 2010). All Rights Reserved

J.B. Davis, *Statistics Using SAS® Enterprise Guide®* (Copyright SAS Institute Inc., Cary, NC, USA, 2007). All Rights Reserved

G. Der, B.S. Everitt, *Basic Statistics Using SAS® Enterprise Guide®: A Primer* (Copyright SAS Institute Inc., Cary, NC, USA, 2007). All Rights Reserved

P.J. Diggle, *Time Series: A Biostatistical Introduction* (Oxford University Press, Oxford, 1990)

W.H. Greene, *Econometric Analysis*, 7th edn. (Pearson, London, 2012)

R.J. Hyndman, G. Athanasopoulos, *Forecasting: Principles and Practice*, 2nd edn. (OTexts, 2018)

K. Kakamu, H. Wago, Small-sample properties of panel spatial autoregressive models: comparison of the Bayesian and maximum likelihood methods. Spat. Econ. Anal. **3**(3), 305–319 (2008)

S. Liu, On diagnostics in conditionally heteroskedastic time series models under elliptical distributions. J. Appl. Probab. **41A**, 393–405 (2004)

S. Liu, T. Ma, W. Polasek, Spatial system estimators for panel models: a sensitivity and simulation study. Math. Comput. Simul. **101**, 78–102 (2014)

Y. Liu, G. Ji, S. Liu, Influence diagnostics in a vector autoregressive model. J. Stat. Comput. Simul. **85**(13), 2632–2655 (2015)

Y. Liu, R. Sang, S. Liu, Diagnostic analysis for a vector autoregressive model under Student-t distributions. Stat. Neerl. **71**(2), 86–114 (2017)

L.S. Meyers, G. Gamst, A.J. Guarino, *Data Analysis Using SAS Enterprise Guide* (Cambridge University Press, Cambridge CB2 8RU, UK, 2009)

A. Milhøj, *Practical Time Series Analysis Using SAS®* (SAS Institute Inc., Cary, NC, 2013)

A. Milhøj, *Multiple Time Series Modeling Using the SAS® VARMAX Procedure* (SAS Institute Inc., Cary, NC, 2016)

O. Parr-Rud, *Business Analytics Using SAS® Enterprise Guide® and SAS® Enterprise Miner™: A Beginner's Guide* (Copyright SAS Institute Inc., Cary, NC, USA, 2014). All Rights Reserved

R.H. Shumway, D.S. Stoffer, *Time Series Analysis and Its Applications*, 3rd edn. (Springer, Berlin, 2011)

S.J. Slaughter, L.D. Delwiche, *The Little SAS® Enterprise Guide® Book* (Copyright SAS Institute Inc., Cary, NC, USA, 2017). All Rights Reserved

J.M. Wooldridge, *Introductory Econometrics: A Modern Approach*, 6th edn. (Cengage, Boston, 2016)

F. Zhu, L. Shi, S. Liu, Influence diagnostics in log-linear integer-valued GARCH models. AStA Adv. Stat. Anal. **99**, 311–335 (2015)

F. Zhu, S. Liu, L. Shi, Local influence analysis for poisson autoregression with an application to stock transaction data. Stat. Neerl. **70**, 4–25 (2016)

Chapter 2
Basic Statistics and Regression Models

Abstract Basic statistical analysis and linear regression modelling techniques are the most important tools for any data analytics and predictive modelling exercise. In this chapter, we will introduce how basic statistical tasks such as descriptive statistics summaries and plots, tests for normality and data transformations can be conducted in SAS EG. In addition, we will cover simple and multiple linear regression, with numerical examples to illustrate how these can be conducted in SAS EG.

Keywords Cross sectional data · Descriptive statistics · Line plot · Linear regression · Normality test · Panel data · Scatter plot · Time series data · Transformation

2.1 Basic Statistics

2.1.1 Data Types

There are a number of different types of data which can be explored and used. In this book, we focus on the following three types: cross sectional, time series and panel data.

Cross Sectional Data

In cross sectional data, the observations are collected across a sample of individuals at the same point in time. A simple example is the collection of students' marks on the same assignment. Another example is the CLASS data in the SASHELP Library, which contains the age, height and weight observations of the students in a class collected at the same point in time (maybe the same day or same week).

Time Series Data

In time series data, the observations are collected for the same individual or variable over a period of equal time intervals. For example, we may have the number of tourists visiting Canberra, Australia in each month for the period 2016–2018, the daily maximum temperatures at the Canberra Airport weather station for the first three months of 2019, or annual Vegemite prices for the years 1995–2011. We have already seen the AIR data set in the SASHELP library which contains the monthly number of passengers for the period Jan 1949–Dec 1960.

Panel Data

In panel data, the observations are collected for the same *sample* of individuals over the same period of equal time intervals. A typical example is the Airline data (Christenson Associates Airline Cost data), which measures the costs, prices of inputs, and utilisation rates for six US airlines over the years 1970–1984. The Airline data is frequently cited, see e.g. Greene (2012) and illustrative examples by the PANEL Procedure in SAS.

2.1.2 Numerical Measures

There are various numerical measures in Statistics which represent or display the descriptive, distributional and/or correlated characteristics of the data under study.

For a sample of n values $x_1, \ldots, x_n$ of the variable of interest X, the sample mean and variance measures are defined as follows.

1. The sample mean is:

$$\overline{x} = \frac{x_1 + \cdots + x_n}{n}$$

2. The sample variance is:

$$s^2 = \frac{(x_1 - \overline{x})^2 + \cdots + (x_n - \overline{x})^2}{n - 1}$$

Provided a sample of n pairs of values $(x_1, y_1), \ldots, (x_n, y_n)$ for the two variables of interest X and Y, the sample covariance and correlation measures are defined as follows.

3. The sample covariance is:

$$s_{xy}^2 = \frac{(x_1 - \overline{x})(y_1 - \overline{y}) + \cdots + (x_n - \overline{x})(y_n - \overline{y})}{n - 1}$$

4. The sample correlation is:

$$r = \frac{s_{xy}^2}{s_x s_y}$$

where s_{xy}^2 is the covariance of variables X and Y, s_x is the standard deviation (i.e. the square-root of the variance) of variable X, and s_y is the standard deviation of variable Y.

Note that the mean, variance, covariance, correlation and other sample statistics can easily be calculated in SAS EG. These calculations can be performed using the following steps.

1. Open the CLASS data from the SASHELP library.

CLASS ▾					
⊞ Filter and Sort ⊞ Query Builder ▼ Where │ Data ▾ Describe ▾ Graph ▾ Analyze ▾ │ Export ▾					
	△ Name	△ Sex	⊛ Age	⊛ Height	⊛ Weight
1	Alfred	M	14	69	112.5
2	Alice	F	13	56.5	84
3	Barbara	F	13	65.3	98
4	Carol	F	14	62.8	102.5
5	Henry	M	14	63.5	102.5
6	James	M	12	57.3	83
7	Jane	F	12	59.8	84.5
8	Janet	F	15	62.5	112.5
9	Jeffrey	M	13	62.5	84
10	John	M	12	59	99.5
11	Joyce	F	11	51.3	50.5
12	Judy	F	14	64.3	90
13	Louise	F	12	56.3	77
14	Mary	F	15	66.5	112
15	Philip	M	16	72	150
16	Robert	M	12	64.8	128
17	Ronald	M	15	67	133
18	Thomas	M	11	57.5	85
19	William	M	15	66.5	112

2. Select **Tasks → Describe → Summary Statistics**, and then in the **Data** option select *Age* as the **Analysis** variable.

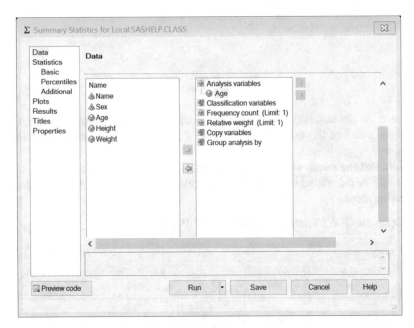

3.   In **Statistics → Basic**, select the required descriptive statistics.

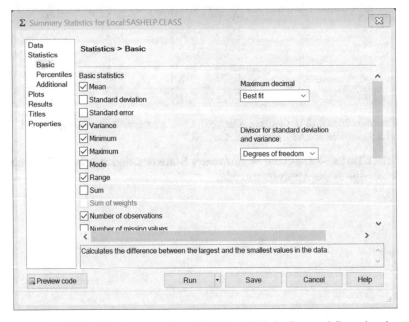

4. Click **Run** to get the numerical results.

   Output 2.1: Summary statistics for *Age* in the CLASS data

   Summary Statistics ▾

   🔲 Input Data 🔲 Code 🔲 Log 🔲 Results
   ⟳ Refresh 🔲 Modify Task | Export ▾ Send To ▾ Create ▾ Publish | 🔲 Properties

   ### Summary Statistics
   ### Results
   #### The MEANS Procedure

Analysis Variable : Age					
Mean	Variance	Minimum	Maximum	Range	N
13.3157895	2.2280702	11.0000000	16.0000000	5.0000000	19

5. To perform a correlation analysis, select **Tasks → Multivariate → Correlations**, and in **Data** select *Height* and *Weight* as the variables, and select the **Pearson** and **Variance** options.

   Output 2.2: Correlation analysis for *Height* and *Weight* in the CLASS data

   ### Correlation Analysis
   #### The CORR Procedure

2 Variables:	Height	Weight

Covariance Matrix, DF = 18		
	Height	Weight
Height	26.2869006	102.4934211
Weight	102.4934211	518.6520468

Simple Statistics						
Variable	N	Mean	Std Dev	Sum	Minimum	Maximum
Height	19	62.33684	5.12708	1184	51.30000	72.00000
Weight	19	100.02632	22.77393	1901	50.50000	150.00000

Pearson Correlation Coefficients, N = 19 Prob > |r| under H0: Rho=0		
	Height	Weight
Height	1.00000	0.87779
		<.0001
Weight	0.87779	1.00000
	<.0001	

We see that the variances, simple statistics, the covariance and the correlation of *Height* and *Weight* are presented in the output. The correlation of 0.87779 is close to 1, indicating that the two variables are strongly and positively associated.

There are many statistical distributions to describe the data or their patterns. The Normal distribution is the most widely used in data analysis and statistics. We often create a histogram, box plot and/or QQ plot of the data under study to help us to roughly see if the data follows a Normal (or another benchmark) distribution—and of course we use these and other plots for additional tasks in analysing and mining data. To be more exact, statistical tests for normality can be conducted and this will be covered later.

In SAS EG, the following steps will create a histogram and QQ plot of the data.

1. Open the CLASS data, select **Tasks → Capability → Histograms** (and then **Tasks → Capability → QQ plot**), and in **Data** select *Age* as the **Analysis** variable.

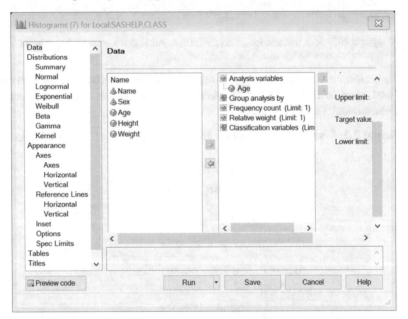

2. Under **Distributions** select "Normal", and then click **Run** to produce the histogram (and QQ plot) of the *Age* variable.

From these plots, we see that the *Age* variable does not seem to follow a Normal distribution well (Figs. 2.1 and 2.2).

While histograms and QQ plots are useful in helping us visually assess the distributional pattern of the data under study, we also need to conduct statistical tests to enhance and confirm our visual assessments. For example, we may use the Shapiro-Wilk or Kolmogorov-Smirnov tests to check statistically if our data follows a Normal distribution. These tests are discussed below.

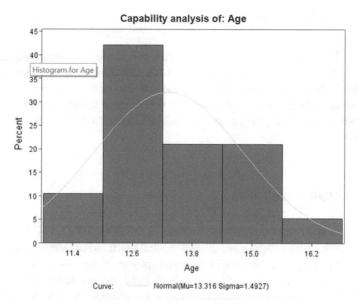

Fig. 2.1 A histogram for *Age* in the CLASS data. Copyright 2019 SAS Institute Inc., Cary, NC, USA. All Rights Reserved. Reproduced with permission of SAS Institute Inc., Cary, NC

Fig. 2.2 A QQ plot for *Age* in the CLASS data. Copyright 2019 SAS Institute Inc., Cary, NC, USA. All Rights Reserved. Reproduced with permission of SAS Institute Inc., Cary, NC

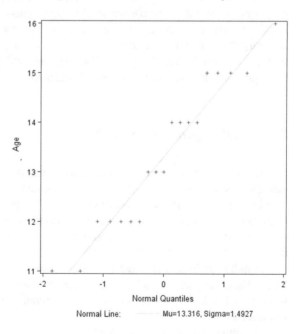

2.2 Normality Tests

Normality is an important concept in Statistics as it is often an underlying distributional assumption of the data set of interest for modelling purposes. For example, after fitting a linear regression we expect the errors to be normally distributed. It is therefore very important to conduct tests to determine if the data satisfies this normality assumption. SAS EG provides several default normality tests. We discuss two of them below.

2.2.1 Shapiro-Wilk Test

The Shapiro-Wilk test was published by Shapiro and Wilk (1965). This test is appropriate for both small sample sizes of up to 50 and much larger sample sizes of up to 2000; see e.g. Meyers et al. (2009). It is perhaps one of the most common tests to assess normality, and can be computed in SAS and a number of other packages.

However, this test also has its disadvantages. For example, it is known to not work well in samples with many identical values.

In this test, the null hypothesis states that the data is normally distributed. If the p value is less than the chosen level of significance α, then the null hypothesis is rejected and there is sufficient evidence to suggest that the data tested is not normally distributed. On the other hand, if the p value is not smaller than the level of significance, then the null hypothesis is not rejected and there is insufficient evidence to suggest that the data is not normally distributed.

2.2.2 Kolmogorov-Smirnov Test

Kolmogorov-Smirnov test is a non-parametric test that can be used to compare the distributions of two data sets or samples, or one sample with a reference probability distribution. The Kolmogorov-Smirnov test can be modified to serve as a goodness of fit test. In the special case of testing the distribution for normality, samples are standardized and compared with a standard normal distribution. This test works best in samples with more than 2000 observations; see e.g. Meyers et al. (2009).

The null hypothesis states that the sample comes from a certain probability distribution with a specific cumulative distribution function (cdf) F_1. Here, it can test whether our sample data set comes from a population that follows the Normal Distribution.

If the maximum absolute difference D_n:

$$D_n = \sup_{-\infty < x < \infty} \left| \hat{F}_n(x) - F_1(x) \right|$$

between F_1 and the sample cdf $\hat{F}_n$ is small, the test does not reject the null hypothesis and suggests that there is insufficient evidence to conclude that the sample data set does not come from a population that follows a Normal distribution.

The Kolmogorov-Smirnov test is invariant under transformations; however, its main weakness is detecting distribution tail discrepancies. There are two refined tests: the Anderson-Darling and the Cramer von-Mises tests; see e.g. Anderson and Darling (1954) and Meyers et al. (2009). These two tests, particularly the Anderson-Darling, are more sensitive to the tails of distributions than specified, and are hence generally considered to be more powerful than the original Kolmogorov-Smirnov test.

2.2.3 Numerical Example

The STEEL dataset available in SAS EG presents the annual iron and steel exports in millions of tonnes from 1937 to 1980 for the US. To conduct the above normality tests in SAS EG:

1. Select **Describe** → **Distribution Analysis**.
2. In the **Data** tab, select the *STEEL* variable as the **Analysis variable**.

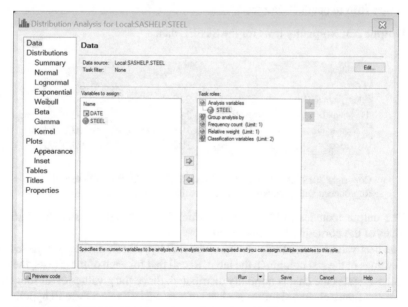

3. In the **Tables** tab, tick the **Tests for normality** box.

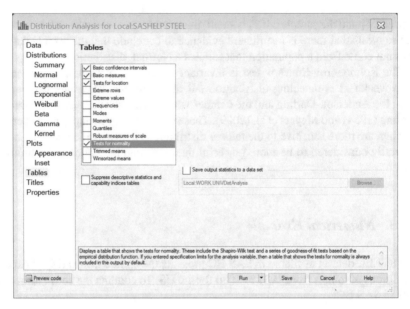

4. Click **Run** to conduct four tests.

Output 2.3: Normality tests for the STEEL data

Tests for Normality				
Test	Statistic		p Value	
Shapiro-Wilk	W	0.919216	Pr < W	0.0045
Kolmogorov-Smirnov	D	0.141097	Pr > D	0.0260
Cramer-von Mises	W-Sq	0.193053	Pr > W-Sq	0.0063
Anderson-Darling	A-Sq	1.202077	Pr > A-Sq	<0.0050

The output includes the table above which includes the test statistics and the p values of the normality tests discussed.

The best values to use to determine if the null hypothesis should be rejected are the p values in the last column in the table. Recall that for each of these tests, the null hypothesis states the data is normally distributed. Since the p values of all four tests are smaller than a chosen significance level of $\alpha = 5\%$, we reject the null hypothesis. We conclude that there is sufficient evidence at this level of significance to suggest that the data is not normally distributed.

2.3 Transforming Data

Computing new variables by applying a mathematical operation is particularly useful for data transformations. When computed in SAS EG, the result of the transformation is calculated in a new column. For example, the distribution of a salary variable for a randomly selected sample may be right-skewed. We may consider taking the logarithm transformation of the salary variable and then examining if the log-transformed values follow a Normal distribution using the normality tests.

Note that the new variables do not have to be formal transformations and can simply be newly calculated statistics (e.g. z-scores) which we discuss below.

2.3.1 z-scores

Once the normality assumption is satisfied, the z-score can be calculated using the following formula:

$$z = \frac{X - \bar{x}}{s}$$

The z-score z indicates how many standard deviations (s) an observation X in a sample is from the sample mean $\bar{x}$. It is a good statistic to use when comparing observations to their sample mean.

2.3.2 Numerical Example

The AIR data available in SAS EG represents the number of airline passengers every month from January 1949 to December 1960. A plot of the time series is presented below (Fig. 2.3).

We see that the data is heteroskedastic, with the variability increasing over time. This presents a potential problem for statistical analysis and model-fitting. To address the heteroskedasticity, a log transformation can be taken. The steps to perform the log transformation are presented below.

1. Click **Query Builder**.

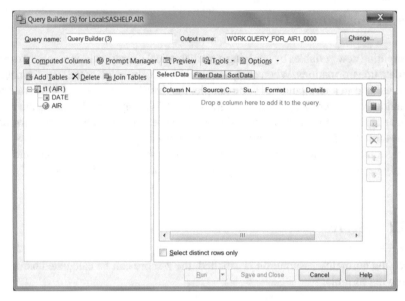

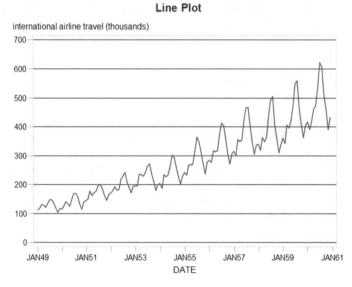

Fig. 2.3 A time series plot of the AIR dataset ('000 passengers, Jan 1949–Dec 1960). Copyright 2019 SAS Institute Inc., Cary, NC, USA. All Rights Reserved. Reproduced with permission of SAS Institute Inc., Cary, NC

2. Click **Computed Columns**.

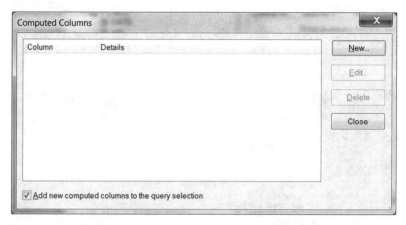

3. Click **New** and select the **Advanced expression** option.

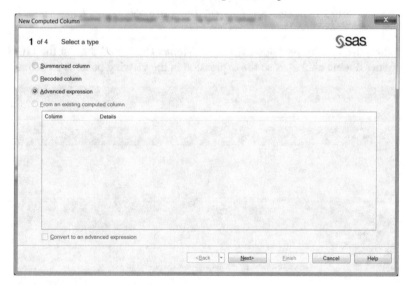

4. Click **Next**. In the bottom left panel, open the **Function** folder and double-click the LOG10 function.

5. Close the **Functions** folder. Open the **Tables** folder and then in the **t1(AIR)**
    folder double click *AIR* so the expression in the viewing panel is as below.

6. Click **Next**. Call the Column Name "log(AIR)".

7. Click **Finish** to get:

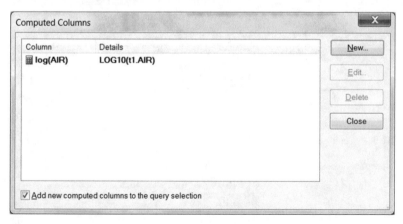

8. Click **Close** to get:

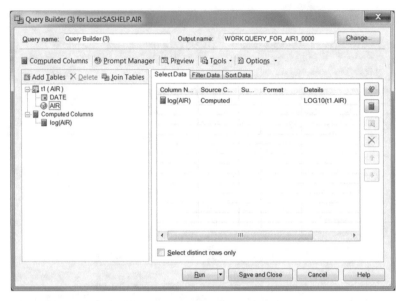

9.   Drag all the other variables (*DATE* and *AIR*) into the right panel to get:

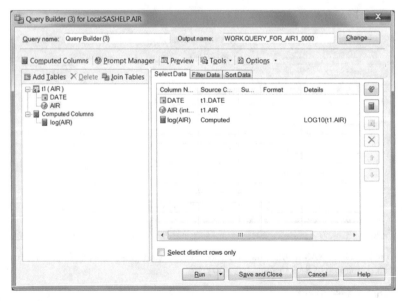

10.   Click **Run** to get the following output data.

Query Builder (3) ▾

	DATE	AIR	log(AIR)
1▸	JAN49	112	2.0492180227
2	FEB49	118	2.0718820073
3	MAR49	132	2.1205739312
4	APR49	129	2.1105897103
5	MAY49	121	2.0827853703
6	JUN49	135	2.1303337685
7	JUL49	148	2.1702617154
8	AUG49	148	2.1702617154
9	SEP49	136	2.1335389084
10	OCT49	119	2.0755469614
11	NOV49	104	2.0170333393
12	DEC49	118	2.0718820073

A plot of the transformed data shows that the heteroskedasticity problem has been reduced (Fig. 2.4).

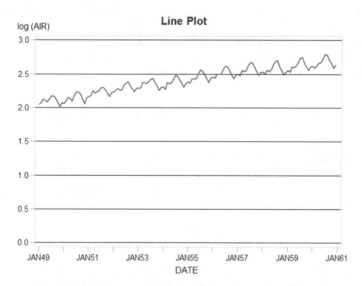

Fig. 2.4 A time series plot of the log transformation of the AIR data ('000 passengers, Jan 1949–Dec 1960). Copyright 2019 SAS Institute Inc., Cary, NC, USA. All Rights Reserved. Reproduced with permission of SAS Institute Inc., Cary, NC

2.4   Simple Linear Regression

Simple linear regression is a statistical technique that fits a linear relationship between two variables: the explanatory variable (X) and the dependent variable (Y). The explanatory variable is the variable that will affect the dependent variable, which is the variable of interest. For example, if we are interested in how income will be affected by the number of hours worked, income would be the dependent variable and the number of hours worked would be the explanatory variable.

2.4.1   Fitting Model Parameters

The simple linear regression model for the population (from which a sample of n data points are collected) can be denoted as:

$$Y_i = \beta_0 + \beta_1 X_i + u_i$$

where Y_i is the observed response value for an individual or object i, X_i is the explanatory variable, β_0 and β_1 are the intercept and slope parameters respectively, and u_i is the error in the model ($i = 1, \ldots, n$) . In our brief example above, Y_i would denote the ith observation of the income variable and X_i would denote the ith observation of the number of hours worked variable.

Simple linear regression relies on, among others, a method called least squares estimation. The method assigns a distance function:

$$d\left(\hat{\beta}_0, \hat{\beta}_1\right) = \sum_{i=1}^{n}(Y_i - \hat{Y}_i)^2 = \sum_{i=1}^{n}(Y_i - \hat{\beta}_0 - \hat{\beta}_1 X_i)^2,$$

which is the sum of squared residuals i.e. the sum of the squared distances between any observed data point and the fitted regression line. The parameter estimates that minimise this distance function (the sum of squared residuals) are $\hat{\beta}_0$ and $\hat{\beta}_1$. The fitted regression line is then:

$$\hat{Y}_i = \hat{\beta}_0 + \hat{\beta}_1 X_i$$

Such a fitted linear model with the least squares concept can be illustrated by the following figure taken from Wooldridge (2016) which presents a scatter plot with fitted values and residuals used in least squares (Fig. 2.5).

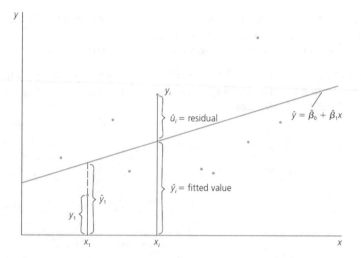

Fig. 2.5 An example of fitted values and residuals. *Source* Wooldridge (2016, Fig. 2.4)

2.4.2 Checking Model Assumptions

When fitting a simple linear regression model, there are a number of assumptions involved. After fitting the model, it is important to check that these assumptions are satisfied. In this book, we focus on the following assumptions underlying the errors of a simple linear regression model:

- The errors are independent.
- The errors are identically distributed with zero mean and equal variance (i.e. homoskedastic).
- The errors are normally distributed.

These assumptions can be written as:

$$u_i \sim N\left(0, \sigma^2\right).$$

These key assumptions can be checked by examining the residual plots, as shown in the example below.

2.4.3 Numerical Example

The CLASS dataset available in SAS EG provides information about a small class of students. Information is collected on the students' sex, age, height and weight. In this example, a simple linear regression is conducted to examine the relationship between height and weight. The question of interest is how height (the explanatory variable) affects weight (the dependent variable).

The steps to create a scatter plot in SAS EG are presented below.

1. Select **Graph → Scatter Plot… → 2D Scatter Plot → Data → Run**.
2. In the **Data** tab, drag the *Weight* variable under **Vertical** and drag the *Height* variable under **Horizontal**.

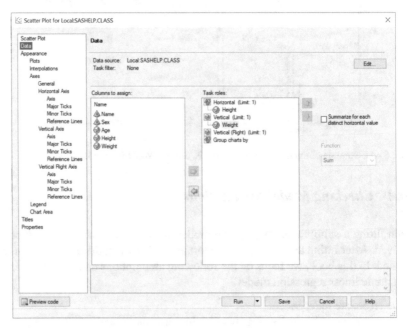

3. Click **Run**.

We now obtain a scatter plot as presented below (Fig. 2.6):

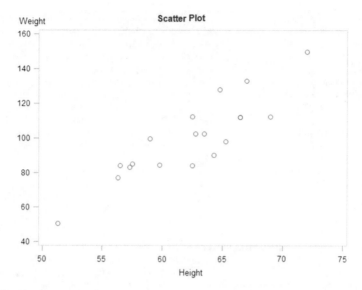

Fig. 2.6 A scatter plot of *Weight* against *Height* for the CLASS data. Copyright 2019 SAS Institute Inc., Cary, NC, USA. All Rights Reserved. Reproduced with permission of SAS Institute Inc., Cary, NC

The scatter plot indicates that a linear relationship is appropriate and the relationship between *Weight* and *Height* is positive and strong. No outliers are observed, and it seems appropriate to fit a linear model to this data.

The steps to fitting a simple linear regression model are presented below.

1. Click **Tasks → Regression → Linear regression**…
2. In the **Data** tab, drag the *Weight* variable under **Dependent variable** and drag the *Height* variable under **Explanatory variables**.

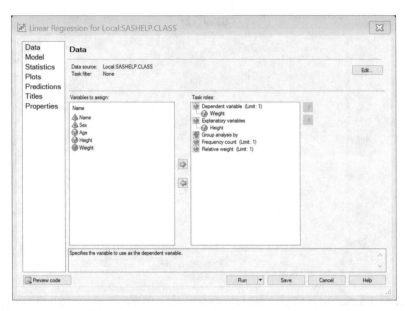

3. In the **Model** tab, it is possible to select a model selection method from the drop-down menu. These model selection methods allow us to fit the most statistically significant model when given a large number of explanatory variables. Since we are only interested in one explanatory variable in this example, leaving this at the default option is fine.

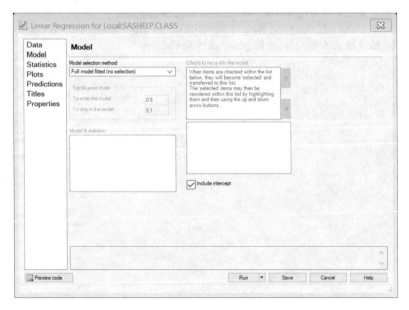

4.   In the **Statistics** tab, estimates and diagnostics of interest can be produced, such
as:

   a.   variance inflation values—these determine if multicollinearity exists (the
presence of high correlations between explanatory variables).

   b.   heteroskedasticity tests—this determines if the data is heteroskedastic.

5.   In the **Plots** tab, plots of interest such as the diagnostic plots for assessing model
assumptions and a scatter plot superimposed with the fitted regression line can
be created. Select the **Custom list of plots** option and tick the **Diagnostic plot**
and **Scatter plot with regression line** boxes.

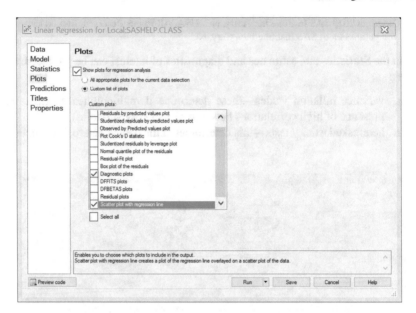

6. Click **Run** to produce the simple linear regression results.

Note that these regression results are actually produced by the REG Procedure in SAS (behind the scenes); for an online illustrative example of implementing the REG Procedure in the SAS code, visit the SAS Support website listed in Appendix A.2. The results are presented in Outputs 2.4–2.6 below with commentary.

Output 2.4: Simple linear regression output for the CLASS data

Linear Regression Results

The REG Procedure
Model: Linear_Regression_Model
Dependent Variable: Weight

Number of Observations Read	19
Number of Observations Used	19

Analysis of Variance					
Source	DF	Sum of Squares	Mean Square	F Value	Pr > F
Model	1	7193.24912	7193.24912	57.08	<.0001
Error	17	2142.48772	126.02869		
Corrected Total	18	9335.73684			

Root MSE	11.22625	R-Square	0.7705
Dependent Mean	100.02632	Adj R-Sq	0.7570
Coeff Var	11.22330		

Parameter Estimates					
Variable	DF	Parameter Estimate	Standard Error	t Value	Pr > |t|
Intercept	1	-143.02692	32.27459	-4.43	0.0004
Height	1	3.89903	0.51609	7.55	<.0001

The Analysis of Variance (ANOVA) table conducts an F test, which compares the explained variation in the model to the unexplained variation, giving us an F value. The null hypothesis of the F test states that the model is not statistically significant. If the p value for this test is smaller than the level of significance, then there is more explained variation relative to the unexplained variation and the overall model is statistically significant. In this example, the p value is less than 0.0001 and the null hypothesis is rejected, suggesting that there is sufficient evidence to conclude that the model is statistically significant.

The table below the ANOVA table provides us with some important measures:

- Root MSE (root mean square error) is the square root of the Mean Square Error figure in the ANOVA table $\left(\sqrt{126.02869} = 11.22625\right)$. The lower this measure is, the more precise the model parameter estimates are.
- Dependent Mean is the mean of the response variable.
- Coeff Var (coefficient of variation) is the ratio of the root MSE to the dependent mean multiplied by 100 $\left(\frac{11.22625}{100.02632} \times 100 = 11.2233\right)$. It represents the relative fit of the model to the data, compared to other models. A lower coefficient of variation indicates a better fit to the data.

- R-Square (R^2 or coefficient of determination) is the proportion of variation in the response variable that can be explained by the model involving the predictor variables. It is the Regression Sum of Squares divided by the Total Sum of Squares $\left(\frac{7193.24912}{9335.73684} = 0.7705\right)$. A higher R^2 would suggest more explained variation in the model and a more suitable model for prediction purposes. In this example, 77.05% of the variation in *Weight* is explained by this model involving *Height*. This is a moderately high R^2 value.
- Adj R-Sq (adjusted R^2) is the same as the regular R^2 except it has been adjusted for the number of degrees of freedom. This allows it to be compared between models when looking for the best model with the 'greatest explanatory power'. The adjustment in this example leads to a slight decrease in the proportion of variation explained, from 0.7705 to 0.7570.

The bottom table displays the parameter estimates of the model, calculated by using the least squares method as discussed previously. From this information, the equation of the fitted regression model is:

$$\widehat{\text{Weight}} = -143.02692 + 3.89903\,\text{Height}$$

From this fitted regression equation, each unit increase in *Height* results in an expected increase in *Weight* by 3.89903 units.

The t value is the test statistic for the t test, which tests if the intercept and slope coefficients are significant (i.e. if they are different from 0). Formally, the null hypothesis can be written as $H_0: \beta_0 = 0$ or $H_0: \beta_1 = 0$. The p values for these tests are also given, and since both are small, the null hypothesis can be rejected. The conclusion is that both the intercept and slope estimates are significantly different from 0.

Output 2.5: Simple linear regression diagnostics output

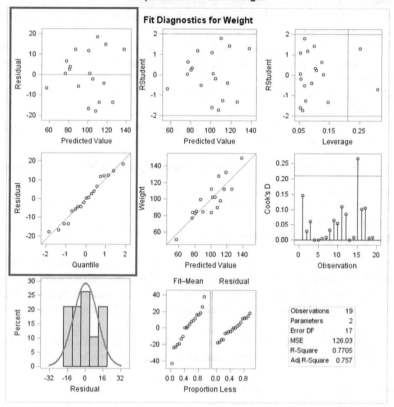

Linear Regression Results

The REG Procedure
Model: Linear_Regression_Model
Dependent Variable: Weight

The above plots are the diagnostics plots which can be used to assess if the assumptions of the model are satisfied.

Moving from left to right within each row and then down each row, each of the plots is briefly discussed below.

1. The Residual versus Predicted Value plot displays the pattern of the residuals against the predicted or fitted values. Linearity, independence and homoskedasticity can be assessed with this plot.
2. The RStudent versus Predicted Value plot displays the Studentised residuals against the predicted values. This plot reveals the same insights as the first plot, but uses Studentised residuals on the vertical axis.

3. The RStudent versus Leverage plot displays the Studentised residuals versus the leverage values. This plot identifies outliers and observations with high leverage in the model. There are two observations with leverage values above the benchmark.
4. The QQ plot indicates the residuals approximately follow a Normal distribution as the observations are close to the straight line.
5. The Weight versus Predicted Value plot displays the observed weights versus the predicted weights. The observations follow the straight line, indicating the regression model fits reasonably well.
6. Cook's Distance plot identifies observation 15 as an observation with high influence.
7. The histogram is not as useful as the QQ plot when determining if the residuals follow a Normal distribution.

Recall that the three main assumptions underlying simple linear regression are:

1. The errors are independent.
2. The errors are identically distributed with zero mean and constant variance (homoskedastic).
3. The errors are normally distributed.

From the Residual plot and the QQ plot (circled above), there is no strong evidence suggesting the model assumptions are not satisfied. The Residual plot shows a random scatter of observations with constant spread, indicating assumptions 1 and 2 are satisfied. The QQ plot shows that the observations roughly follow the straight line, indicating assumption 3 is satisfied.

The plot below is the scatter plot of *Weight* against *Height* with the fitted regression line superimposed. The 95% confidence and prediction intervals are also shown by default.

Output 2.6 Simple regression prediction results

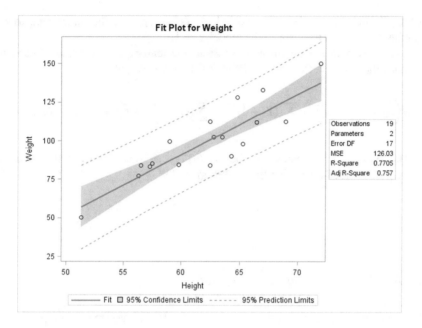

Fit Plot for Weight

Observations	19
Parameters	2
Error DF	17
MSE	126.03
R-Square	0.7705
Adj R-Square	0.757

The prediction interval is always wider than the confidence interval. This is because the prediction interval is the interval which is likely to contain the next sampled response observation from the population (which is more variable), whereas the confidence interval is the interval estimate of the mean response (which is less variable). The prediction interval includes the random error of a new observation, and is hence based on a larger standard error than the confidence interval. Note that the point prediction and the point estimate at a particular x value under both intervals are numerically the same (as given by the fitted line).

2.5 Multiple Linear Regression

Multiple Linear Regression is an extension of simple linear regression, where there are multiple explanatory variables which affect the response variable.

2.5.1 Fitting Model Parameters

The multiple linear regression model for the population is:

$$Y_i = \beta_0 + \beta_1 X_{i1} + \beta_2 X_{i2} + \cdots + \beta_k X_{ik} + u_i$$

where Y_i and X_i are the observed values, $\beta_0, \ldots, \beta_k$ are the parameters to be estimated, and u_i is the error in the model, $i = 1, \ldots, n$.

Again, as with simple linear regression, the least-squares method is used to estimate the parameters. Now the distance function is defined as:

$$d\left(\hat{\beta}_0, \hat{\beta}_1, \ldots, \hat{\beta}_k\right) = \sum_{i=1}^{n}(Y_i - \hat{Y}_i)^2 = \sum_{i=1}^{n}(Y_i - \hat{\beta}_0 - \hat{\beta}_1 X_{i1} - \cdots - \hat{\beta}_k X_{ik})^2$$

The parameter estimates will be $\hat{\beta}_0, \hat{\beta}_1, \ldots, \hat{\beta}_k$ that minimise the distance function. The fitted regression line is then given by:

$$\hat{Y}_i = \hat{\beta}_0 + \hat{\beta}_1 X_{i1} + \hat{\beta}_2 X_{i2} + \cdots + \hat{\beta}_k X_{ik}$$

2.5.2 Checking Model Assumptions

The assumptions underlying the errors from a multiple linear regression model are the same that apply to simple linear regression:

1. The errors are independent.
2. The errors are identically distributed with zero mean and constant variance (homoskedastic).
3. The errors are normally distributed.

In other words, $u_i \sim N\left(0, \sigma^2 I\right)$. These key assumptions can be checked by examining the diagnostic plots as with simple linear regression.

2.5.3 Numerical Example

We return to the CLASS dataset available in SAS EG. In this example, a multiple linear regression is conducted to analyse the relationship between *Height, Age* and *Weight* by fitting a multiple linear regression model. We are interested in how *Height* and *Age* affect *Weight*.

1. Select **Analyze → Regression → Linear regression**…
2. In the **Data** tab, drag the *Weight* variable under **Dependent variable** and drag the *Age* and *Height* variables under **Explanatory variables**.

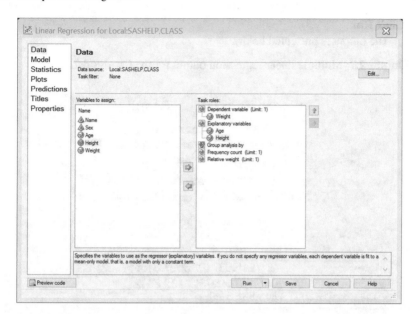

3. In the **Plots** tab, select the **Custom list of plots** option and tick the **Diagnostic plots** box. A scatter plot cannot be drawn here as the model involves two explanatory variables.

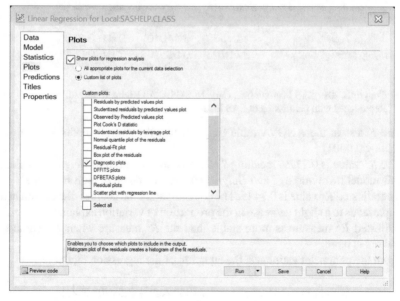

4. Click **Run**.

The output is presented below.

Output 2.7: Multiple linear regression output for the CLASS data

Linear Regression Results

The REG Procedure
Model: Linear_Regression_Model
Dependent Variable: Weight

Number of Observations Read	19
Number of Observations Used	19

Analysis of Variance					
Source	DF	Sum of Squares	Mean Square	F Value	Pr > F
Model	2	7215.63710	3607.81855	27.23	<.0001
Error	16	2120.09974	132.50623		
Corrected Total	18	9335.73684			

Root MSE	11.51114	R-Square	0.7729
Dependent Mean	100.02632	Adj R-Sq	0.7445
Coeff Var	11.50811		

Parameter Estimates					
Variable	DF	Parameter Estimate	Standard Error	t Value	Pr > |t|
Intercept	1	-141.22376	33.38309	-4.23	0.0006
Age	1	1.27839	3.11010	0.41	0.6865
Height	1	3.59703	0.90546	3.97	0.0011

The F test in the ANOVA table suggests that the overall model is significant (p value < 0.0001).

The R^2 value is 0.7729, meaning 77.29% of the variation in *Weight* is explained by this model involving *Age* and *Height*. This is a moderately high R^2 value.

The adjusted R^2 value is 0.7445. The adjustment for the degrees of freedom in this example leads to a slight decrease in the proportion of variation explained. Generally, the adjusted R^2 measure is more stable than the R^2 measure when the number of predictors is large.

From the parameter estimates, the equation of the regression model is:

$$\widehat{\text{Weight}} = -141.22376 + 1.27839\,\text{Age} + 3.59703\,\text{Height}$$

When *Age* increases by one unit and *Height* is held constant, *Weight* is expected to increase by 1.27839 units. When *Height* increases by one unit and *Age* is held constant, *Weight* is expected to increase by 3.59703 units.

The *t* tests conclude that while the intercept and the slope estimate for the *Height* variable are significantly different from 0, the slope estimate for the *Age* variable is not significantly different from 0. Therefore the *Age* variable is not a statistically significant predictor of *Weight*.

Output 2.8: Multiple linear regression diagnostics output

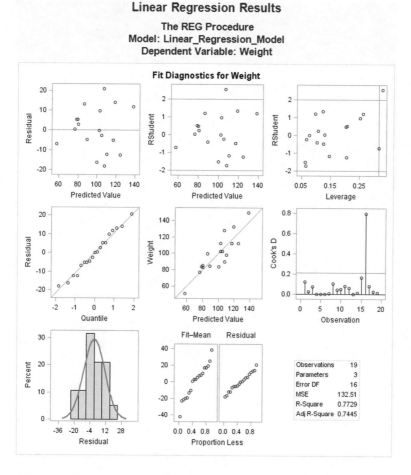

From the diagnostic plots, it appears the model assumptions are satisfied.

References

T.W. Anderson, D.A. Darling, A test of goodness-of-fit. J. Am. Stat. Assoc. **49**, 765–769 (1954)

L.S. Meyers, G. Gamst, A.J. Guarino, *Data Analysis Using SAS Enterprise Guide* (Cambridge University Press, Cambridge CB2 8RU, UK, 2009)

S.S. Shapiro, M.B. Wilk, An analysis of variance test for normality (complete samples). Biometrika **52**(3–4), 591–611 (1965)

J.M. Wooldridge, *Introductory Econometrics: A Modern Approach*, 6th edn. (Cengage, Boston, 2016)

Chapter 3
Basic Forecasting

Abstract A time series is a set of numerical data collected at regular intervals over time, to be denoted $Y_t (t = 1, \ldots, T)$ hereafter. The data may be collected annually, semi-annually or monthly. The goal of time series analysis is to use historical data patterns to create a model which can then be used for forecasting. The analysis usually consists of three components: descriptive analysis, modelling and forecasting. In the descriptive analysis stage, the data is observed over time to find a long-term trend. In the modelling stage, a model is fitted to the data based on the properties in the data. For forecasting, the model derived in the modelling stage is used to predict future values. In this chapter, we will discuss the descriptive analysis stage and focus on the moving average smoothing and exponential smoothing methods to identify the long-term trend. We will then discuss the modelling and forecasting stages in Chap. 4.

Keywords Exponential smoothing · Forecasting · Long-term trend · Moving average smoothing

3.1 Descriptive Analysis

The first step in time series analysis is to identify the long-term trend in the data. However, there may not always be a long-term trend present, or it may be difficult to identify one.

The Unemployed Persons data set from the Australian Bureau of Statistics (Labour Force, Australia, Detailed, Cat. No. 6291.0.55.003) contains the number of unemployed persons from the hospitality industry each year from 1995 to 2007; see also Berenson et al. (2013).

Figure 3.1 presents a line plot of the Unemployed Persons data.

Electronic supplementary material The online version of this chapter
(https://doi.org/10.1007/978-981-15-0321-4_3) contains supplementary material, which is
available to authorized users.

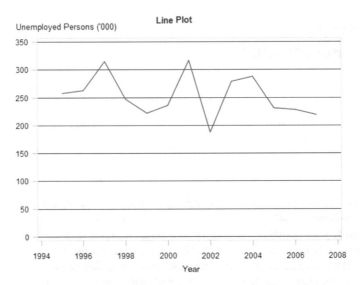

Fig. 3.1 A time series plot of Unemployed Persons from the hospitality industry ('000 people, 1995–2007). Copyright 2019 SAS Institute Inc., Cary, NC, USA. All Rights Reserved. Reproduced with permission of SAS Institute Inc., Cary, NC

In the graph above, it may be difficult to determine if a long-term trend is present. To aid in the trend identification, it is possible to smooth out short term fluctuations in the series using the moving average method or the exponential smoothing method, which are two common smoothing techniques and covered in basic statistics and business analytics; see e.g. Berenson et al. (2013) and Black et al. (2019). We will discuss these two methods below.

3.2   Smoothing Methods

Moving Average

Moving averages contain a series of averages calculated over time such that each average takes into account L time periods. Moving averages are denoted as $MA(L)$, where L represents the number of time periods taken into account for each calculation of the average.

As an example, suppose we want to compute five-year moving averages from a series Y_t that has $T = 11$ years ($t = 1, 2, \ldots, 11$). Since $L = 5$, the five-year moving averages contain a series of averages computed by averaging consecutive sequences of five values. To calculate the first five-year moving average, sum the values of the first five years in the series and divide by 5:

$$MA(5) = \frac{Y_1 + Y_2 + Y_3 + Y_4 + Y_5}{5}$$

To find the second five-year moving average, sum the values of the second year to the sixth year in the series and divide by 5:

$$MA(5) = \frac{Y_2 + Y_3 + Y_4 + Y_5 + Y_6}{5}$$

Continue this process until the last of these five-year moving averages is calculated by summing the values of the last five years in the series (i.e. the seventh year through to the eleventh year) and then dividing by 5:

$$MA(5) = \frac{Y_7 + Y_8 + Y_9 + Y_{10} + Y_{11}}{5}$$

This results in a series of five-year moving averages which can be plotted to show the long-term trend of the series.

Exponential Smoothing

Exponential smoothing involves calculating exponentially weighted values using previous observations. The equation developed for exponentially smoothing a series Y_t in any time period, t, is based on the current value in the time series, the previously computed exponentially smoothed value, and an assigned weight or smoothing coefficient, W. The equation below is used to exponentially smooth a time series.

$$E_1 = Y_1$$
$$E_t = WY_t + (1 - W)E_{t-1} \tag{3.1}$$

where E_t is the value of the exponentially smoothed series being calculated in time period t, E_{t-1} is the value of the exponentially smoothed series already calculated in time period $t - 1$, Y_i is the observed value of the time series in time period t, and W is a subjectively assigned smoothing coefficient, where $0 < W < 1$ and $t = 2, 3, 4, \ldots, T$.

The choice of the smoothing coefficient W can be subjective, however there are some guidelines to what is suitable depending on our goal. If our goal is to just smooth a series by eliminating unwanted cyclical and irregular variations, a small value for W (close to 0) should be selected. This ensures the overall trend of the series becomes more noticeable. If our goal is forecasting, a large value for W (close to 1) should be chosen. This allows future short-term directions to be sufficiently predictable.

Exponential smoothing allows us to conduct short term forecasting. The exponentially smoothed value for the current period can be the forecast for the consecutive one.

Then we have the following one-step-ahead forecast for time period $t + 1$:

$$\hat{Y}_{t+1} = E_t \tag{3.2}$$

3.2.1 Numerical Example

The Vegemite Price data represents the cost of a 375 g jar of Vegemite from 1995 to 2011; see Berenson et al. (2013). The data is given below. In this example, we will smooth the data and identify the long-term trend using the moving average and exponential smoothing methods.

1. Import the data:

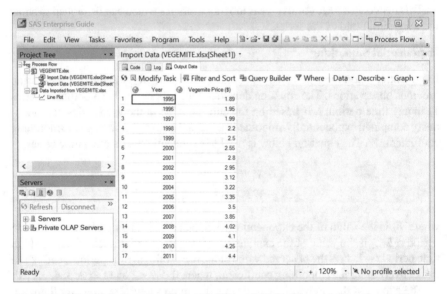

2. Plot the data to get a visual representation of the data. Click **Graph → Line Plot** to get:

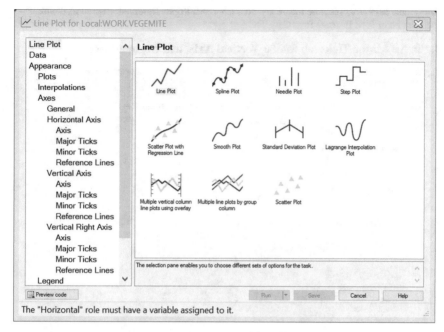

3. In the **Data** tab, drag *Year* under **Horizontal** and *Vegemite Price* ($) under **Vertical**:

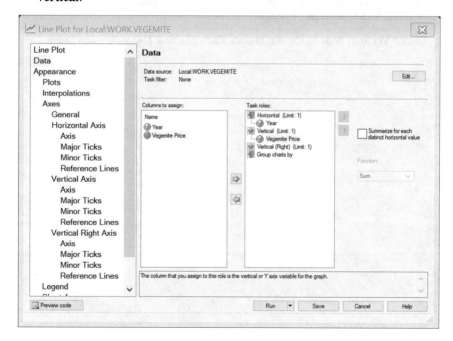

4.   In the **Major Ticks** tab for the **Vertical Axis**, tick **Begin at zero**:

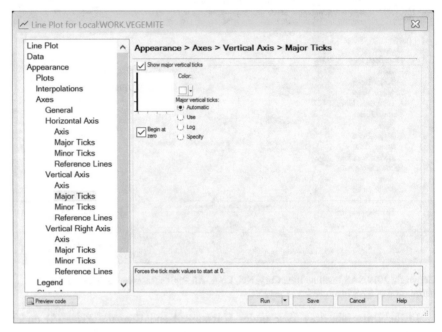

5.   Under **Vertical Axis** in the **Reference lines** tab, tick **Use reference lines**:

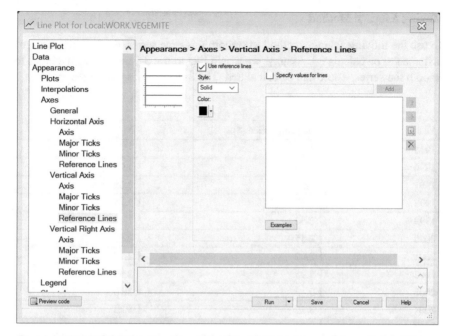

6.   Click **Run** to produce the line plot (Fig. 3.2):

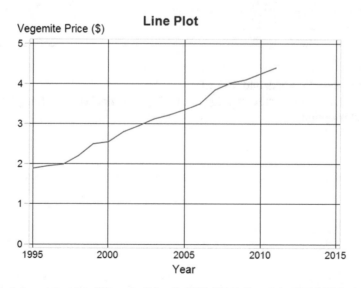

Fig. 3.2   A time series plot of Vegemite Price ($, 1995–2011). Copyright 2019 SAS Institute Inc., Cary, NC, USA. All Rights Reserved. Reproduced with permission of SAS Institute Inc., Cary, NC

Moving Average Method

To use the moving average method to smooth this time series, the moving averages first need to be calculated. Assume we would like to use 3-year moving averages to smooth the series. These can be calculated. The 3-year moving averages are:

Year	Vegemite price ($)	MA(3)
1995	1.89	
1996	1.95	1.94
1997	1.99	2.05
1998	2.20	2.23
1999	2.50	2.42
2000	2.55	2.62
2001	2.80	2.77
2002	2.95	2.96
2003	3.12	3.10
2004	3.22	3.23
2005	3.35	3.36
2006	3.50	3.57
2007	3.85	3.79
2008	4.02	3.99
2009	4.10	4.12
2010	4.25	4.25
2011	4.40	

1. Import the above data into SAS EG.
2. Create a line plot of the data using the **Multiple vertical column line plot using overlay** option.

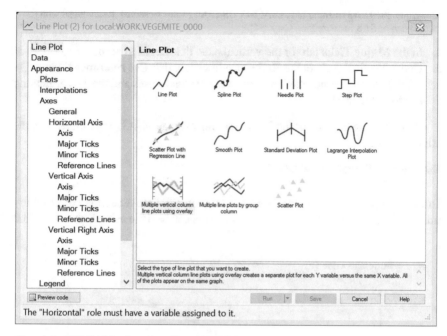

3. In the **Data** tab, drag *Year* under **Horizontal**, and *Vegemite Price ($)* and *MA(3)* under **Vertical**:

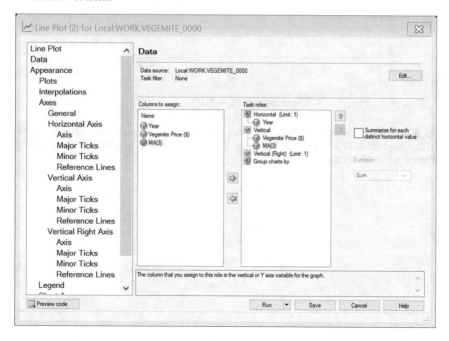

4. In the **Major Ticks** tab for the vertical axis, tick **Begin at zero**.
5. Under **Vertical Axis** in the **Reference lines** tab, tick **Use reference lines**.
6. Click **Run** to produce the line plot of the original series and the 3-year moving
    average (Fig. 3.3).

Obviously, the line plot of the 3-year moving average MA(3) is smoother than the
original series.

Exponential Smoothing Method

To use the exponential smoothing method to smooth this time series, the exponentially
smoothed values need to be calculated first. This can be done using Eqs. 3.1 and 3.2

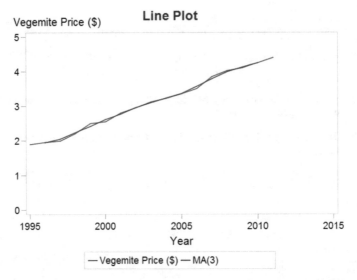

Fig. 3.3 A time series plot of Vegemite Price with 3-year moving average values ($, 1995–
2011). Copyright 2019 SAS Institute Inc., Cary, NC, USA. All Rights Reserved. Reproduced with
permission of SAS Institute Inc., Cary, NC

presented previously. We will assume a smoothing coefficient of $W = 0.5$ to smooth the series. The calculated exponentially smoothed values are:

Year	Vegemite price ($)	ES ($W = 0.5$)
1995	1.89	1.89
1996	1.95	1.92
1997	1.99	1.96
1998	2.20	2.08
1999	2.50	2.29
2000	2.55	2.42
2001	2.80	2.61
2002	2.95	2.78
2003	3.12	2.95
2004	3.22	3.08
2005	3.35	3.22
2006	3.50	3.36
2007	3.85	3.60
2008	4.02	3.81
2009	4.10	3.96
2010	4.25	4.10
2011	4.40	4.25

1. Import the above data into SAS EG.
2. Create a line plot of the data using the **Multiple vertical column line plot using overlay** option.
3. In the **Data** tab, drag *Year* under **Horizontal**, and *Vegemite Price ($)* and *ES (W = 0.5)* under **Vertical**.
4. In the **Major Ticks** tab for the vertical axis, tick **Begin at zero**.
5. In the **Reference lines** tab for the vertical axis, tick **Use reference lines**.
6. Click **Run** to produce the line plot of the original series and the exponentially smoothed series (Fig. 3.4).

We see that the exponentially smoothed line is heavily influenced by the initial value. As the 1995 price of $1.89 is lower than the 1996 price of $1.95, the exponentially smoothed line is consistently below the original series. This is because, as per the definition in Eqs. 3.1 and 3.2, the smoothed value is the weighted average of the previously smoothed value and the current observation.

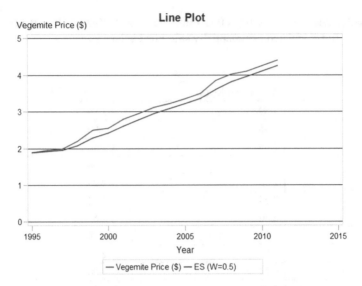

Fig. 3.4 A time series plot of Vegemite Price with exponentially smoothed values ($, 1995–2011). Copyright 2019 SAS Institute Inc., Cary, NC, USA. All Rights Reserved. Reproduced with permission of SAS Institute Inc., Cary, NC

References

M.L. Berenson, D.M. Levine, T.C. Krehbiel, D.F. Stephan, M. O'Brien, N. Jayne, J. Watson, *Basic Business Statistics: Concepts and Applications*, 3rd edn. (Pearson, London, 2013)
K. Black, J. Asafu-Adjaye, P. Burke, N. Khan, G. King, N. Perera, A. Papadimos, C. Sherwood, S. Wasimi, *Business Analytics and Statistics* (Wiley, Hoboken, 2019)

Chapter 4
ARIMA Modelling and Forecasting

Abstract The Auto-Regressive Integrated Moving Average (ARIMA) model is the general class of models for modelling and forecasting a time series. It consists of the AR, MA and ARMA models. In this chapter, we will discuss each of these models in turn before summarising the steps for ARIMA modelling. We conclude this chapter with a numerical example.

Keywords Augmented Dickey-Fuller test · Autocorrelation function · Auto-regressive · Auto-regressive integrated moving average · Auto-regressive moving average · Moving average · Lag · Stationarity

4.1 Auto-Regressive (AR) Model

The AR model is a technique used to forecast time series that display autocorrelation (where the values of a time series are highly correlated with the past observations). The auto-regressive model is denoted AR(p), where p is the order of the model and represents the number of past observations that affect the current value of the series. The model equation is given as:

$$Y_t = A_0 + A_1 Y_{t-1} + A_2 Y_{t-2} + \cdots + A_p Y_{t-p} + \varepsilon_t \tag{4.1}$$

where Y_t is the observed value of the series at time t, Y_{t-h} is the observed value of the series at time $t-h$ with lag h, A_h is the autoregression parameter to be estimated, and ε_t is a non-autocorrelated random error with zero mean and constant variance, $t = 1, \ldots, T$ and $h = 1, \ldots, p$.

Electronic supplementary material The online version of this chapter (https://doi.org/10.1007/978-981-15-0321-4_4) contains supplementary material, which is available to authorized users.

4.2   Moving Average (MA) Model

The MA model explains the relationship between Y_t and past error terms. It is denoted MA(q), where q represents the number of past error terms that affect the current value of the series. The model equation is given as:

$$Y_t = \varepsilon_t + B_1 \varepsilon_{t-1} + B_2 \varepsilon_{t-2} + \cdots + B_q \varepsilon_{t-q} \qquad (4.2)$$

where Y_t is the observed value of the series at time t, ε_t is a non-autocorrelated random error with zero mean and constant variance at time t, ε_{t-k} is a non-autocorrelated random error with zero mean and constant variance at time $t - k$, and B_k is the autoregression parameter to be estimated, $t = 1, \ldots, T$ and $k = 1, \ldots, q$.

4.3   Auto-Regressive Moving Average (ARMA) Model

The ARMA process incorporates both AR and MA models. The current value of the series therefore depends on past observations and past errors. The model is denoted ARMA(p, q), where p and q represent the same items as in AR and MA models discussed previously.

$$\begin{aligned} Y_t = A_1 Y_{t-1} + A_2 Y_{t-2} + \cdots + A_p Y_{t-p} + \varepsilon_t \\ + B_1 \varepsilon_{t-1} + B_2 \varepsilon_{t-2} + \cdots + B_q \varepsilon_{t-q} \end{aligned} \qquad (4.3)$$

where $A_1, A_2, \ldots, A_p$ are the quantified impacts of $Y_{t-1}, Y_{t-2}, \ldots, Y_{t-p}$ on Y_t, and $B_1, B_2, \ldots, B_q$ are the quantified impacts of $\varepsilon_{t-1}, \varepsilon_{t-2}, \ldots, \varepsilon_{t-q}$ on Y_t.

An ARMA model may be replaced by an autoregressive integrated moving average model, denoted by ARIMA (p, d, q) where d is the order of integration. When qualities of non-stationarity are shown in the data, an initial differencing step (corresponding to the "integrated" part of the model) can be applied one or more times to eliminate the non-stationarity. Stationarity is covered in detail in the next section.

For example, if Y_t is not stationary, we consider the differenced series $\Delta Y_t = Y_t - Y_{t-1}$. If ΔY_t is stationary, the order of integration is $d = 1$ and we may fit ΔY_t by using an ARMA(p, q) model or fit Y_t using an ARIMA(p, 1, q) model. If ΔY_t is still not stationary, we need to find $\Delta^2 Y_t = \Delta Y_t - \Delta Y_{t-1}$. If $\Delta^2 Y_t$ is stationary, the order of integration is $d = 2$ and we can fit it using an ARMA(p, q) model or fit Y_t using an ARIMA(p, 2, q) model.

Note that the AR(p), MA(q) and ARMA(p, q) models in Eqs. (4.1), (4.2) and (4.3) are all special cases of the general ARIMA (p, d, q) model. They can be alternatively denoted as ARIMA(p, 0, 0), ARIMA(0, 0, q) and ARIMA(p, 0, q), respectively. For detailed discussions on these models, see e.g. Ajmani (2009), Brocklebank et al. (2018) and Hyndman and Athanasopoulos (2018).

In the next few sections we discuss the ARIMA(p, d, q) modelling steps, including a more detailed discussion on stationarity.

4.4   Steps in ARIMA Modelling

The main steps in ARIMA modelling are:

1. Test the time series for stationarity.

   a. If the series is non-stationary, take differences of the time series to achieve stationarity.

2. Identify the model to fit the now stationary time series.
3. Estimate the parameters of the chosen model.
4. Forecast with the model.

The numerical example at the end of the chapter will go through each of the above steps. Firstly, we will cover the theoretical aspects of each step.

Step 1: Test for stationarity

A time series is stationary if:

- its mean is constant (e.g. no trend),
- its variance is constant (i.e. homoskedastic), and
- if periodic variations have been eliminated.

A stationary time series is in a state of equilibrium. A stationary series is easier to model as the series only fluctuates within certain limits and the previous or future values of the mean and variance of the series are not exceptionally different. It is not easy to identify patterns in a non-stationary time series, so checking for stationarity is crucial for model building.

The AIR data discussed previously has often been used as an example of a non-stationary seasonal time series. In addition, Fig. 4.1 showing Retail Turnover data from the Australian Bureau of Statistics (Retail Trade Trends, Australia, Cat. No. 8501.0) and Berenson et al. (2013) is a simple example of a non-stationary series, with an obvious trend i.e. unequal mean over time.

As the non-stationary series grows, the values of the series start inflating too much. It becomes difficult to predict the series using the ARIMA approach in such a case. Many real-life scenarios result in non-stationary series. A transformation may need to be applied or the series may need to be differenced to make it stationary. We will cover the details of differentiation later.

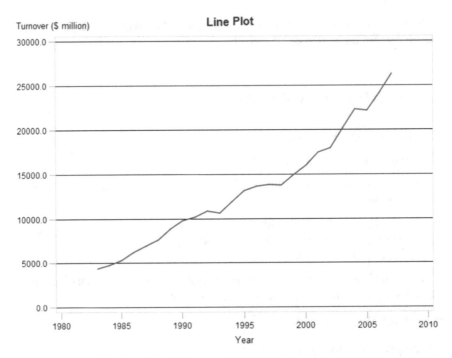

Fig. 4.1 A time series plot of Retail Turnover (1983–2007). Copyright 2019 SAS Institute Inc., Cary, NC, USA. All Rights Reserved. Reproduced with permission of SAS Institute Inc., Cary, NC

Figure 4.2 shows a stationary time series. Some steadiness is apparent, and there is no obvious increasing or decreasing trend. The variance and mean of the series also show steadiness or a state of equilibrium. However, we cannot conclude based on appearance that this series is stationary. We need a scientifically proven statistical approach to test for stationarity and this is discussed in the next section.

Testing for Stationarity Using the Augmented Dickey-Fuller Test

To test if the series is stationary, we may use the Dickey-Fuller (DF) or Augmented Dickey-Fuller (ADF) tests, among others. The actual theory behind DF and ADF tests will not be covered in detail in this book; see e.g. Wooldridge (2016) and Brocklebank et al. (2018) for details. SAS EG has capabilities to perform the ADF test (when lag $= 0$ then this becomes a DF test), so the basics of the tests for practical use in SAS EG are given below.

The null and alternative hypotheses of the ADF test are:

- H_0: The series is not stationary
- H_1: The series is stationary

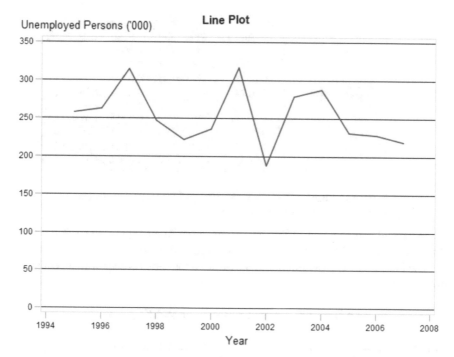

Fig. 4.2 A time series plot of Unemployed Persons ('000 people, 1995–2007). Copyright 2019 SAS Institute Inc., Cary, NC, USA. All Rights Reserved. Reproduced with permission of SAS Institute Inc., Cary, NC

If the p value from the test is less than the level of significance, say $\alpha = 0.05$ as commonly used, we reject the null hypothesis and conclude that there is sufficient evidence to suggest the series is stationary. On the other hand, if the p value is higher than the level of significance, we do not reject the null hypothesis and conclude that there is insufficient evidence to suggest the series is stationary.

To conduct an ADF Test for the AIR data in SAS EG, we proceed as follows:

1. Go to **Analyze → Time Series → ARIMA Modelling and Forecasting...**
2. In the **Stationarity Tests** tab, select to perform an ADF test to produce the following output.

   Output 4.1: ADF test results for the AIR data

Augmented Dickey-Fuller Unit Root Tests							
Type	Lags	Rho	Pr < Rho	Tau	Pr < Tau	F	Pr > F
Zero Mean	0	0.0628	0.6961	0.05	0.6968		
	1	-0.6525	0.5367	-0.35	0.5561		
	2	-0.0086	0.6796	-0.01	0.6797		
Single Mean	0	-5.8727	0.3515	-1.75	0.4050	1.85	0.6002
	1	-11.2712	0.0932	-2.35	0.1594	2.93	0.3240
	2	-7.2580	0.2524	-1.81	0.3739	1.91	0.5830
Trend	0	-38.3509	0.0007	-4.64	0.0013	10.76	0.0010
	1	-122.232	0.0001	-7.65	<.0001	29.28	0.0010
	2	-165.906	0.0001	-7.09	<.0001	25.11	0.0010

In general, we may look at the three types of the Augmented Dickey-Fuller Unit Root Tests in the table above and select one type to focus on.

The Zero Mean type assumes that the mean of the series is zero with an equation form such as:

$$\Delta Y_t = \rho\, Y_{t-1} + \gamma_1 \Delta Y_{t-1} + \cdots + \gamma_p \Delta Y_{t-p} + \varepsilon_t$$

where $\Delta Y_{t-h} = Y_{t-h} - Y_{t-h-1}$ is the difference between the observed value at time $t - h$ and its lag ($h = 1, \ldots, p$), and ε_t is the error at time t.

The Single Mean type assumes that the series is stationary involving some non-zero constant mean in general (or with a zero mean for the Zero Mean type, which is a special case) with an equation form such as:

$$\Delta Y_t = \mu + \rho\, Y_{t-1} + \gamma_1 \Delta Y_{t-1} + \cdots + \gamma_p \Delta Y_{t-p} + \varepsilon_t$$

where μ is the mean.

The Trend type assumes that the series is stationary involving both some non-zero constant mean and a trend component with an equation form such as:

$$\Delta Y_t = \mu + \phi\, t + \rho\, Y_{t-1} + \gamma_1 \Delta Y_{t-1} + \cdots + \gamma_p \Delta Y_{t-p} + \varepsilon_t$$

where t is the time trend.

The ADF test output has the following sets of p values:

- The Zero Mean p values are higher than a significance level of $\alpha = 0.05$ for lags 0, 1, and 2.
- The Single Mean p values are higher than a significance level of $\alpha = 0.05$ for lags 0, 1, and 2.
- In contrast, the Trend p values are lower than a significance level of $\alpha = 0.05$ for lags 0, 1, and 2.

Hence, for the Zero Mean and Single Mean types, we cannot reject the null hypothesis H_0 and therefore conclude that there is insufficient evidence to suggest that the series under consideration is stationary; this seems to be due to the trend involved in the data. For the Trend type, there is sufficient evidence to conclude that the de-trended series is stationary.

Note that Wooldridge (2016) discusses the Tau values which are compared to the corresponding critical values tabulated for the Zero Mean, Single Mean and Trend types. Brocklebank et al. (2018) covers the three tests involving the Rho, Tau and F values.

Achieving Stationarity

If a series is not stationary, it can be differentiated to achieve stationarity. If Y_t is the original series, then the differenced series is calculated as $\Delta Y_t = Y_t - Y_{t-1}$ for each observation. This differenced series can then be tested for stationarity. Sometimes a series needs to be differentiated more than once before it becomes stationary.

Differencing can be done in SAS EG:

1. Go to **Analyze** $\rightarrow$ **Time Series** $\rightarrow$ **ARIMA Modelling and Forecasting...**
2. Select it in the **Differencing** tab.

Step 2: Identify the model

Model identification is one of the important steps in time series modelling using the ARIMA approach. The aim of model identification is to determine the type of series we are dealing with (whether it is AR or MA or ARMA), and then the order of the series (whether it is AR(1) or AR(2) or MA(1) or ARMA(1,2) etc.). The final forecast accuracy will depend on the identification of the correct model.

Identifying the model is not easy. It is not enough to look at the plot of the series and conclude the type and order of the series. The autocorrelation function (ACF) and partial autocorrelation function (PACF) plots are two useful tools to help identify the type and order of the series. These will be discussed in the following sections.

Autocovariance Function (γ_h)

The autocovariance function represents the covariance between Y_t and Y_{t-h}, where h indicates the lag. It is denoted as γ_h. Usually, when the covariance is calculated, it is calculated between two separate variables. However, in this case the covariance is calculated between Y and its previous values. Note the autocovariance is a function of h but not t (assumed to be the same for every time t under stationarity, $t = 1, \ldots, T$).

For example, for an AR(1) series of the form:

$$Y_t = \rho Y_{t-1} + \epsilon_t$$

where $|\rho| < 1$ and ϵ_t is the error with mean 0 and variance σ^2, the covariance sequence is:

$$\gamma_h = \frac{\rho^{|h|}\sigma^2}{1-\rho^2}$$

where $|.|$ indicates the absolute value.

For a general AR(p), MA(q) or ARMA(p,q) series, γ_h is presented by e.g. Brocklebank et al. (2018).

Autocorrelation Function (ACF)

The autocorrelation function refers to the correlation between Y_t and Y_{t-h}, and is denoted by ρ_h. It is then a function of lag h, specifically the normalized autocovariance:

$$\rho_h = \frac{\gamma_h}{\gamma_0}$$

where γ_h is the autocovariance between Y_t and Y_{t-h}, and γ_0 is the variance of Y_t, $t = 1, \ldots, T$ and $h = 1, \ldots, p$.

Note that $\rho_0 = 1$ for all series and $\rho_h = \rho_{-h}$.

For example:

- ACF(0): Correlation at lag 0 (ρ_0) = Correlation between Y_t and Y_t. Thus, $\rho_0 = 1$.
- ACF(1): Correlation at lag 1 (ρ_1) = Correlation between Y_t and Y_{t-1}.
- ACF(2): Correlation at lag 2 (ρ_2) = Correlation between Y_t and Y_{t-2}.
- ACF(3): Correlation at lag 3 (ρ_3) = Correlation between Y_t and Y_{t-3}.

The graphs created using the autocorrelation values are called autocorrelation plots. Figure 4.3 shows an example of such a plot. The x-axis represents the lag values, while the y-axis represents the autocorrelation values. The graph might vary based on the type of the series.

Fig. 4.3   An example of an ACF plot. Copyright 2019 SAS Institute Inc., Cary, NC, USA. All Rights Reserved. Reproduced with permission of SAS Institute Inc., Cary, NC

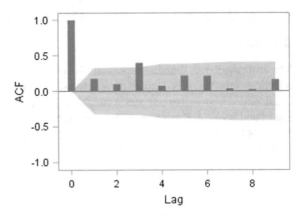

Partial Autocorrelation Function (PACF)

The partial autocorrelation function calculates the partial correlations between Y and its previous values at different lags. The partial correlation is the correlation after removing the effect of the other variables. The PACF is denoted by θ_h, where h indicates the lag, and is given by:

$$
\begin{pmatrix}
\gamma_0 & \cdots & \gamma_{h-1} \\
\vdots & \ddots & \vdots \\
\gamma_{h-1} & \cdots & \gamma_0
\end{pmatrix}
\begin{pmatrix}
\theta_1 \\
\vdots \\
\theta_h
\end{pmatrix}
=
\begin{pmatrix}
\gamma_1 \\
\vdots \\
\gamma_h
\end{pmatrix}
$$

It can be found by regressing the previous values of Y on the current value. For example:

- PACF(0): Partial correlation at lag 0 $(\theta_0) = 1$.
- PACF(1): Partial correlation at lag 1 (θ_1) = Regression coefficient of Y_{t-1} when Y_{t-1} is regressed on Y_t.
- PACF(2): Partial correlation at lag 2 (θ_2) = Regression coefficient of Y_{t-2} when Y_{t-1} and Y_{t-2} are regressed on Y_t.
- PACF(3): Partial correlation at lag 3 (θ_3) = Regression coefficient of Y_{t-3} when Y_{t-1}, Y_{t-2} and Y_{t-3} are regressed on Y_t.

The graphs created using partial autocorrelation values are called partial autocorrelation plots. Figure 4.4 shows an example of such a plot. The x-axis represents the lag values, while the y-axis represents the partial autocorrelation values. As is the case with ACF, a PACF graph might vary based on the type of series.

Rules of Thumb for Identifying the AR Process

When the ACF plot shows a reducing tendency toward zero, the process is an AR process. The PACF plot then needs to be inspected to determine the order of the

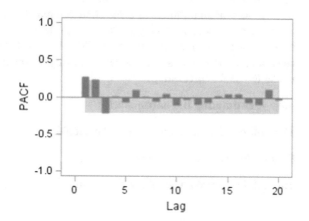

Fig. 4.4 An example of a PACF plot. Copyright 2019 SAS Institute Inc., Cary, NC, USA. All Rights Reserved. Reproduced with permission of SAS Institute Inc., Cary, NC

series. The PACF plot cuts off for an AR process and the lag number at which the PACF plot cuts off is the order of the series.

For example, if the ACF plot slowly tails off towards zero and the PACF plot cuts off at lag 1, then the order of the AR process is 1. If the ACF plot tails off to zero and the PACF plot cuts off at lag 2, then the order of the AR process is 2.

Rules of Thumb for Identifying the MA Process

The method of identifying the MA process is very similar to identifying the AR process. However, for an MA process the PACF plot slowly tails off, and the ACF plot cuts off. The lag at which the ACF plot cuts off is the order of the MA series.

Note that because the MA process deals with errors, which are generally small in magnitude, the PACF plot is not always clear and may be hard to interpret. The inverse autocorrelation function (IACF) plot can be used as a substitute in this case. Therefore a MA process is characterized by the PACF or IACF plot tailing off to zero and the lag at which the ACF plot cuts off is the order of the series.

Inverse Autocorrelation Function (IACF)

The inverse autocorrelation function is an autocorrelation function where the roles of errors are interchanged with the actual series values. The ACF plot for ARMA(2,0) looks the same as an IACF plot for ARMA(0,2). The IACF is similar to an autocorrelation function calculated between the errors. The IACF can be used as a substitute to PACF in the analysis. For some models such as a MA process, an IACF plot shows a clearer trend and is hence easier to interpret.

Rules of Thumb for Identifying the ARMA Process

In comparison to identifying pure AR and pure MA processes, it may not be easy to identify the orders of an ARMA process. If the ACF plot diminishes to zero, then it is an AR process and the PACF plot gives the order of the AR process. If the IACF or PACF plot diminishes to zero, then it is a MA process and the order is determined by looking at the ACF plot. For an ARMA process, the ACF, PACF, and IACF plots will all diminish to zero. Though it may be quick to identify the process as an ARMA process, it may be difficult to determine the orders of the process by looking at the ACF, PACF, and IACF plots. Instead, AIC or BIC values can be compared between various models with varying orders to decide on the optimal model to use for forecasting.

Step 3: Estimating the parameters

This will be covered in the numerical example.

Step 4: Forecasting with the model

This will be covered in the numerical example.

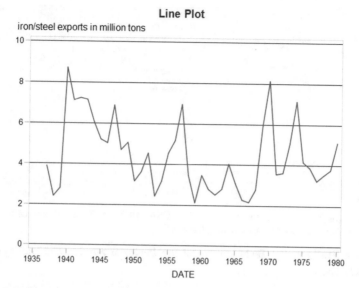

Line Plot

Fig. 4.5 A time series plot of iron and steel exports (million tonnes, 1937–1980). Copyright 2019 SAS Institute Inc., Cary, NC, USA. All Rights Reserved. Reproduced with permission of SAS Institute Inc., Cary, NC

4.4.1   Numerical Example

We recall that the STEEL dataset in the SAS library represents the annual iron and steel exports in millions of tonnes from 1937 to 1980 for the US. Our aim is to fit an appropriate model to this dataset. It is always useful to plot the data first:

1. Click **Graph → Line** Plot to create a line plot.
2. In the **Data** tab, select the variables.
3. In the **Major Ticks** tab for the vertical axis, tick **Begin at zero**.
4. In the **Reference lines** tab for the vertical axis, tick **Use reference lines**.
5. Click **Run** to produce the line plot (Fig. 4.5).

Step 1: Determine if the series is stationary

From the line plot, it appears the series is stationary as it seems stable with no trend. We can use the ADF Test to test this.

1. Go **Tasks → Time Series → ARIMA Modelling and Forecasting…**
2. In the **Data** tab, select the *STEEL* variable as the Time Series variable and *DATE* as the Time ID variable.

3. In the **Stationarity Tests** tab, select the **Perform augmented Dickey-Fuller
    tests** option

4. Click **Run** to get the test output.

    Output 4.2: ADF test results for the STEEL data

Augmented Dickey-Fuller Unit Root Tests							
Type	Lags	Rho	Pr < Rho	Tau	Pr < Tau	F	Pr > F
Zero Mean	0	-2.8498	0.2416	-1.15	0.2238		
	1	-1.9403	0.3337	-0.87	0.3330		
	2	-0.9228	0.4814	-0.57	0.4647		
Single Mean	0	-22.6286	0.0022	-3.82	0.0052	7.31	0.0010
	1	-30.4238	0.0003	-3.84	0.0050	7.40	0.0010
	2	-24.5872	0.0010	-3.01	0.0421	4.55	0.0667
Trend	0	-24.2698	0.0112	-3.96	0.0179	7.83	0.0247
	1	-36.0520	0.0002	-4.21	0.0095	8.91	0.0074
	2	-34.7977	0.0002	-3.54	0.0484	6.33	0.0680

This table presents the results for the ADF test for three assumptions: Zero Mean, Single Mean and Trend. The Single Mean and Trend types indicate that the series has a constant non-zero mean and is stationary.

Step 2: Identifying the model

From the output, the following plots have been extracted.

Output 4.3: Plots for trend and correlation analysis

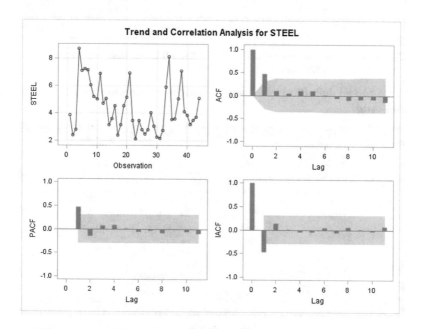

Here, the ACF plot tails off to 0, suggesting the process is an AR model. The PACF plot cuts off at lag 1, indicating it may be an AR(1) model.

On the other hand, we can perceive the PACF plot to be dampening to 0, suggesting it is an MA model. The ACF plot cuts off at lag 1, so it may be an MA(1) model.

We will fit both and then compare summary measures to determine which model is more appropriate.

Step 3: Estimating the parameters

For AR(1):

1. Go **Analyze → Time Series → ARIMA Modelling and Forecasting…**
2. In the **Data** tab, drag the *STEEL* variable under **Time Series variable**.
3. In the **Enable estimating steps** tab, tick the **Perform estimation steps** box.

4. In the **Model definition** tab, enter "1" into the **Factors for the AR Model** and click **Add**.

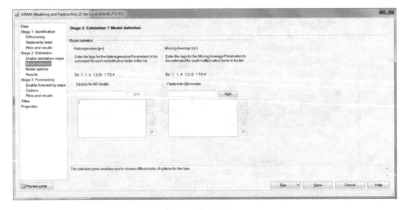

5. Click **Run** to get the following results.

Output 4.4: AR(1) modelling and forecasting results

ARIMA Modeling and Forecasting
Results

The ARIMA Procedure

Name of Variable = STEEL	
Mean of Working Series	4.418182
Standard Deviation	1.73354
Number of Observations	44

Autocorrelation Check for White Noise									
To Lag	Chi-Square	DF	Pr > ChiSq	Autocorrelations					
6	12.15	6	0.0586	0.472	0.104	0.045	0.103	0.099	0.008

Trend and Correlation Analysis for STEEL

Conditional Least Squares Estimation					
Parameter	Estimate	Standard Error	t Value	Approx Pr > |t|	Lag
MU	4.41217	0.43509	10.14	<.0001	0
AR1,1	0.47368	0.13622	3.48	0.0012	1

Constant Estimate	2.322229
Variance Estimate	2.444518
Std Error Estimate	1.563495
AIC	166.149
SBC	169.7174
Number of Residuals	44

* AIC and SBC do not include log determinant.

Correlations of Parameter Estimates		
Parameter	MU	AR1,1
MU	1.000	0.006
AR1,1	0.006	1.000

Autocorrelation Check of Residuals									
To Lag	Chi-Square	DF	Pr > ChiSq	Autocorrelations					
6	2.19	5	0.8224	0.074	-0.151	-0.057	0.072	0.086	-0.020
12	4.32	11	0.9597	-0.020	-0.072	-0.018	-0.006	-0.165	0.046
18	7.29	17	0.9794	0.096	0.013	0.007	-0.061	0.130	-0.102
24	12.95	23	0.9530	-0.216	-0.094	-0.081	-0.039	0.042	-0.050

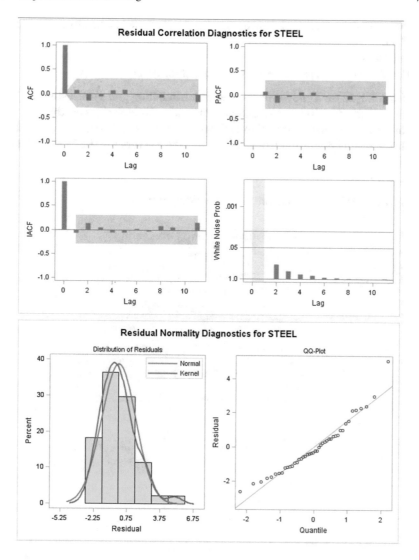

The coefficient table gives the parameter estimates so that the model equation is:

$$\widehat{Y}_t = 4.41217 + 0.47368Y_{t-1}$$

The p value for the AR(1) parameter is very small, indicating it is significantly different from 0. The AIC value is 166.149 and the SBC value is 169.7174.

The residual diagnostics show the ACF and PACF plots tail off to 0, suggesting no residual correlations. The white noise probabilities are also low, indicating there is little unexplained variation remaining. The AR(1) model is therefore a good fit to the data.

For MA(1):

For MA(1), the steps are very similar to that for AR(1):

1. Go **Analyze → Time Series → ARIMA Modelling and Forecasting...**
2. In the **Data** tab, drag the *STEEL* variable under **Time Series variable**.
3. In the **Enable estimating steps** tab, tick the **Perform estimation steps** box.
4. In the **Model definition** tab, enter "1" into the **Factors for the MA Model** and click **Add**.
5. Click **Run**.

Output 4.5: MA(1) modelling and forecasting results

ARIMA Modeling and Forecasting
Results

The ARIMA Procedure

Name of Variable = STEEL	
Mean of Working Series	4.418182
Standard Deviation	1.73354
Number of Observations	44

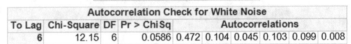

Autocorrelation Check for White Noise								
To Lag	Chi-Square	DF	Pr > ChiSq	Autocorrelations				
6	12.15	6	0.0586	0.472	0.104	0.045	0.103	0.099	0.008

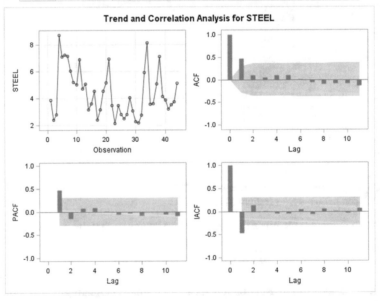

Conditional Least Squares Estimation					
Parameter	Estimate	Standard Error	t Value	Approx Pr > |t|	Lag
MU	4.42102	0.34703	12.74	<.0001	0
MA1,1	-0.49827	0.13512	-3.69	0.0006	1

Constant Estimate	4.421016
Variance Estimate	2.412583
Std Error Estimate	1.553249
AIC	165.5704
SBC	169.1388
Number of Residuals	44

* AIC and SBC do not include log determinant.

Correlations of Parameter Estimates		
Parameter	MU	MA1,1
MU	1.000	-0.008
MA1,1	-0.008	1.000

Autocorrelation Check of Residuals									
To Lag	Chi-Square	DF	Pr > ChiSq	Autocorrelations					
6	1.31	5	0.9336	0.059	0.094	-0.028	0.085	0.075	-0.020
12	3.23	11	0.9873	-0.006	-0.079	-0.052	-0.013	-0.146	0.039
18	6.68	17	0.9874	0.063	-0.001	0.044	-0.092	0.096	-0.149
24	14.00	23	0.9268	-0.206	-0.135	-0.114	-0.084	0.014	-0.072

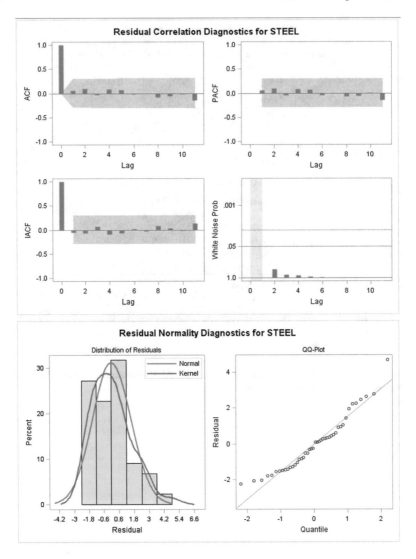

The coefficient table gives the parameter estimates so that the model equation is:

$$\widehat{Y}_t = 4.42102 + \hat{\varepsilon}_t + 0.49827\hat{\varepsilon}_{t-1}.$$

The p value for the MA(1) parameter is very small, indicating it is significant.
The AIC value is 165.5704 and the SBC value is 169.1388.

The residual diagnostics show the ACF and PACF plots tail off to 0, suggesting
no residual correlations. The white noise probabilities are also low, indicating there

is little unexplained variation remaining. The MA(1) model is therefore a good fit to the data.

Comparing the AR(1) and the MA(1) models, we see that:

– The AIC and SBC values for MA(1) are slightly lower, indicating MA(1) is the slightly better model.
– Residual diagnostics are similar, but it appears that MA(1) explains slightly more than the AR(1) model.

Therefore we can conclude the MA(1) model is a slightly better fit to the data and is the better choice for forecasting.

Step 4: Forecasting using the most appropriate model, MA(1)

Ensure the previous steps are followed:

1. Go **Analyze → Time Series → ARIMA Modelling and Forecasting...**
2. In the **Data** tab, drag the *STEEL* variable under **Time Series variable**.
3. In the **Enable estimating steps** tab, tick the **Perform estimation steps** box.
4. In the **Model definition** tab, enter "1" into the **Factors for the MA Model** and click **Add**.
   Now, complete the additional steps below:
5. In the **Enable forecasting steps** tab, tick the **Perform forecasting steps** box.

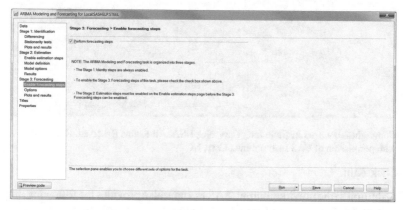

6. In the **Options** tab, and select "Yearly" as the **Time interval between observations** and select the **Number of intervals to forecast** as 5. Leave the **Confidence level** at 95%.

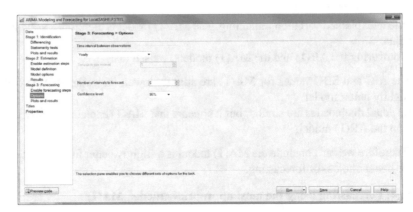

7. In the **Plots and results** tab, tick both the **Forecasts** and **Residuals** boxes.

8. Click **Run**.

In addition to the previous output, SAS EG now also provides the following output.
Output 4.6: Forecasts and confidence limits

Forecasts for variable STEEL				
Obs	Forecast	Std Error	95% Confidence Limits	
45	4.8942	1.5532	1.8499	7.9386
46	4.4210	1.7354	1.0197	7.8223
47	4.4210	1.7354	1.0197	7.8223
48	4.4210	1.7354	1.0197	7.8223
49	4.4210	1.7354	1.0197	7.8223

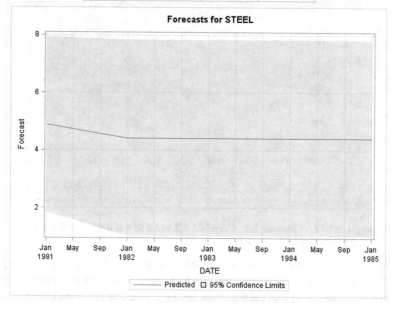

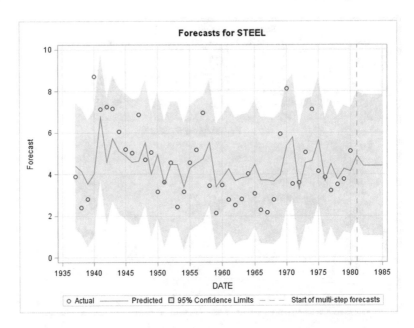

The forecasts for the annual iron and steel exports in millions of tonnes for the next 5 years are given in the first table. The first graph above gives a visual depiction of these forecasts. Note that the forecasts for the 2nd to 5th years are identical. This may be due to the MA(1) model with one-step-ahead forecasts.

The second graph depicts the overall line plot for our current data, including the forecasted values on the right after the vertical dotted line.

Output 4.7: Residual Plots

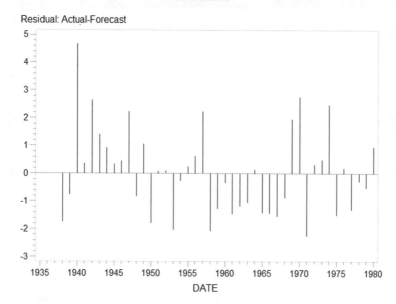

ARIMA Modeling and Forecasting
Residuals

The graph above shows the residuals. Recall that residuals are the difference between the actual observed values and the forecast or predicted values based on the model. If the model is a good fit to the data, we expect the residuals to be random because they represent the irregular component of the time series. The graph above appears random, hence suggesting that the MA(1) is a good fit to the data, as we concluded previously.

References

V.B. Ajmani, *Applied Econometrics Using the SAS® System* (Wiley, Hoboken, 2009)

M.L. Berenson, D.M. Levine, T.C. Krehbiel, D.F. Stephan, M. O'Brien, N. Jayne, J. Watson, *Basic Business Statistics: Concepts and Applications,* 3rd edn. (Pearson, London, 2013)

J.C. Brocklebank, D.A. Dickey, B.S. Choi, *SAS® for Forecasting Time Series*, 3rd edn. (SAS Institute, Cary, NC, 2018)

R.J. Hyndman, G. Athanasopoulos, *Forecasting: Principles and Practice,* 2nd edn. (OTexts, 2018)

J.M. Wooldridge, *Introductory Econometrics: A Modern Approach,* 6th edn. (Cengage, Boston, 2016)

Chapter 5
Regression Analysis with Autoregressive Errors

Abstract In this chapter, we will cover regression models with serially uncorrelated errors and then regression models with autocorrelated (or serially correlated) errors. Why do we need both and especially the latter? When we conduct regression analysis with time series variables, we have to distinguish the two types of scenarios. The first one involves serially uncorrelated errors and accordingly we consider the relevant static models. The second one involves autocorrelation in the errors and so we require the latter. In the latter scenario, the errors are correlated over time, and this is true in many circumstances. This is an obvious violation of the independent errors assumption for linear regression discussed in Chap. 2 so we cannot employ ordinary regression analysis with time series variables in such situations. Instead, the AUTOREG procedure in SAS accounts for the autocorrelation present in the errors and should be utilised to fit a regression model with autoregressive errors.

Keywords Autoregressive errors · Seasonality · Serial correlation · Static time series model · Tests for serial correlation

5.1 Static Time Series Models

Suppose that we have time series data available on the dependent variable y and k predictors, say x_1, ..., x_k, i.e. we have y_t and x_{t1}, ..., x_{tk} dated contemporaneously, $t = 1, \ldots, T$. We define a static model, which can be used to describe the contemporaneous relationship between y and x_1, ..., x_k, as in Wooldridge (2016):

$$y_t = \beta_0 + \beta_1 x_{t1} + \cdots + \beta_k x_{tk} + u_t \tag{5.1}$$

where u_t is an error term at time t, which is often assumed to follow a Normal distribution, $t = 1, \ldots, T$.

Electronic supplementary material The online version of this chapter
(https://doi.org/10.1007/978-981-15-0321-4_5) contains supplementary material, which is available to authorized users.

Static models such as model (5.1) are usually assumed when a change in $x_1, \ldots,$ x_k at time t is believed to have an immediate effect on y, though they are also used when we are interested in understanding the trade-off between y and $x_1, \ldots, x_k$.

Note that the static models are treated in the same way as the classical linear model in terms of estimation and testing. Under the classical linear model assumptions (including normality) for time series, the ordinary least-squares (OLS) estimators are normally distributed and conditional on the predictor values. Furthermore, under the null hypothesis, each t statistic has a t distribution, and each F statistic has an F distribution. The usual construction of confidence intervals is also valid. See Wooldridge (2016, Sect. 10.3, Theorem 10.5) for the details.

5.1.1 Trends and Seasonality

Many economic time series have a tendency to grow or shrink over time. In these cases where there are unobserved factors that are systematically growing or shrinking over time, we can use a time trend as an explanatory variable in our regression to capture the time effect.

When we have seasonally unadjusted data, we can use simple methods to deal with seasonality in regression models in addition to the basic forecasting methods discussed in Chap. 3. In general, we can include a set of seasonal dummy variables to account for seasonality in the dependent variable, the independent variables, or both. For example, with quarterly data we may consider three dummy variables for the four seasons (say Summer, Autumn and Winter). With monthly data we may consider 11 dummy variables for the 12 months (say February–December).

For details on various situations involving different trending and seasonal dummy variables, calculating the corresponding R^2 values and interpreting the relevant results, see e.g. Wooldridge (2016, Sect. 10.5).

5.1.2 Numerical Example

As in Woodridge (2016, Chap. 10) we analyse the Phillips data set, which was compiled from various versions of the *Economic Report of the President* including the *2004 Report* (Tables B-42 and B-64).

In Economics, the Phillips curve explains the relationship between the inflation rate and the unemployment rate. Let's consider the following form of the Phillips curve:

$$inf_t = \beta_0 + \beta_1 unem_t + u_t$$

where inf_t is the annual inflation rate and $unem_t$ is the unemployment rate at time t, where $t = 1, \ldots, T$.

This form assumes a constant natural rate of unemployment and constant inflationary expectations.

We now attempt to fit a model to the PHILLIPS data set, which contains the US inflation and unemployment rates over the years 1948–1996. There are $T = 49$ observations for a number of variables including *unem* and *inf* as in Wooldridge (2016, Sect. 10.3). We proceed with the following steps in SAS EG:

1. Import data by selecting **New Project** and then clicking **File** → **Import Data** to choose our data file named PHILLIPS.xlsx.

2. Select **Tasks** → **Regression** → **Linear Regression** → **Data** to choose *inf* as the **Dependent variable** and *unem* as an **Explanatory variable**.

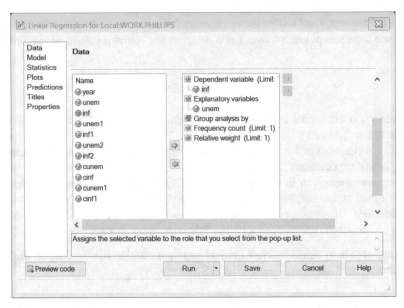

3. Click **Model** with the default option for **Model selection method**.

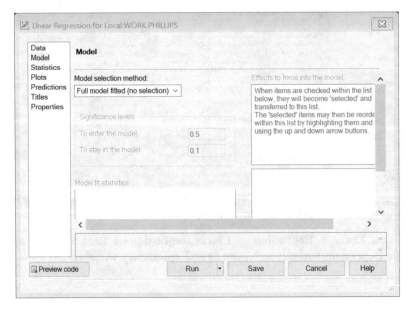

4. Click **Run** to obtain the following output.

Output 5.1: Linear regression output: static Phillips curve

Linear Regression Results

The REG Procedure
Model: Linear_Regression_Model
Dependent Variable: inf

Number of Observations Read	49
Number of Observations Used	49

Analysis of Variance					
Source	DF	Sum of Squares	Mean Square	F Value	Pr > F
Model	1	25.63696	25.63696	2.62	0.1125
Error	47	460.61978	9.80042		
Corrected Total	48	486.25673			

Root MSE	3.13056	R-Square	0.0527
Dependent Mean	4.10816	Adj R-Sq	0.0326
Coeff Var	76.20346		

Parameter Estimates					
Variable	DF	Parameter Estimate	Standard Error	t Value	Pr > |t|
Intercept	1	1.42361	1.71902	0.83	0.4118
unem	1	0.46763	0.28913	1.62	0.1125

The fitted model is:

$$\widehat{inf}_t = 1.4236 + 0.4676\, unem_t$$

with $T = 49$ and $R^2 = 0.0527$.

To determine if there is a trade-off between *unem* and *inf*, we can conduct a hypothesis test with the following hypotheses:

$$H_0: \beta_1 \geq 0$$

$$H_1: \beta_1 < 0$$

We can use the usual OLS t test if the classical linear model (CLM) assumptions hold. As $\hat{\beta}_1 = 0.4676 > 0$ has a p value of 0.1125, which is not less than a level of significance of 5%, the estimated equation does not suggest a trade-off between *unem* and *inf*.

Note that we will investigate if the classical linear model assumptions in this analysis actually hold, and conduct further analysis in the next section.

5.2 Regression Models Involving Serial Correlation

There are various ways in which the error terms can be serially correlated, of which the AR(1) model is the most popular and simplest to study. Assuming a dependent variable y has a relationship with k explanatory variables $x_1, \ldots, x_k$ with an autoregressive AR(1) error process, we have:

$$y_t = \beta_0 + \beta_1 x_{t1} + \cdots + \beta_k x_{tk} + u_t$$
$$u_t = \rho u_{t-1} + \varepsilon_t \tag{5.2}$$

where $|\rho| < 1$ is required for the errors to be stationary, and ε_t are uncorrelated random variables with mean 0 and variance σ^2, though $\varepsilon_t \sim N(0, \sigma^2)$ can be further assumed and then the maximum likelihood estimation (MLE) can be used.

To fit models such as (5.2), we need to test if serial correlation is present in the errors. We discuss the key steps below. For more details, see Wooldridge (2016, Chap. 12).

Testing for AR(1) Serial Correlation

There are a few standard tests for testing for AR(1) serial correlation. Two such tests are the t test and the Durbin-Watson (DW) test available in SAS EG. The null hypothesis of the tests states that the errors are serially uncorrelated:

$$H_0 : \rho = 0$$

How can we test this hypothesis? We can use the AR(1) model:

$$u_t = \rho u_{t-1} + \varepsilon_t$$

and replace u_t with the corresponding OLS residual $\hat{u}_t$ and use the usual t statistic for ρ.

We summarise the asymptotic tests for AR(1) serial correlation below, as taken from Wooldridge (2016, Chap. 12).

Testing for AR(1) Serial Correlation with Strictly Exogenous Regressors:

(1) Run an OLS regression of y_t on $x_{t1}, \ldots, x_{tk}$, which are strictly exogenous (i.e. are uncorrelated with the error term u_t in all time periods), and obtain the OLS residuals $\hat{u}_t$, for all $t = 1, \ldots, T$.
(2) Run a regression of $\hat{u}_t$ on $\hat{u}_{t-1}$, for all $t = 2, \ldots, T$, to obtain the coefficient $\hat{\rho}$ on $\hat{u}_{t-1}$ and its t statistic $t_{\hat{\rho}}$.
(3) Use $t_{\hat{\rho}}$ to test $H_0{:}\rho = 0$ against $H_1{:}\rho \neq 0$ in the usual way (actually, the alternative can be $H_1{:}\rho > 0$ as often expected).

Typically, we conclude that serial correlation is a problem to be dealt with only if H_0 is rejected at the 5% level. As always, it is best to report the p value for the test.

When the explanatory variables are not strictly exogenous, such that one or more x_{tj} are correlated with u_{t-1}, neither the t test introduced above nor the DW statistic are valid, even in large samples. In this case we use one of Durbin's two alternatives to the DW statistic, as discussed by Wooldridge (2016, Chap. 12).

Testing for AR(1) Serial Correlation with General Regressors:

(1) Run an OLS regression of y_t on $x_{t1}, \ldots, x_{tk}$ and obtain the OLS residuals $\hat{u}_t$, for all $t = 1, \ldots, T$.
(2) Run a regression of $\hat{u}_t$ on $x_{t1}, \ldots, x_{tk}, \hat{u}_{t-1}$ for all $t = 2, \ldots, T$ to obtain the coefficient $\hat{\rho}$ on $\hat{u}_{t-1}$ and its t statistic $t_{\hat{\rho}}$.
(3) Use $t_{\hat{\rho}}$ to test $H_0{:}\rho = 0$ against $H_1{:}\rho \neq 0$ in the usual way (or use a one-sided alternative as for strictly exogenous regressors).

In the above equation we regress the OLS residuals on *all* independent variables, including an intercept, and the lagged residual. The t statistic on the lagged residual is a valid test in the AR(1) model.

With quarterly or monthly data that has not been seasonally adjusted, we sometimes wish to test for seasonal forms of serial correlation. With quarterly data, we might postulate an autoregressive model with $\hat{u}_{t-4}$ replacing $\hat{u}_{t-1}$ for the strictly exogenous or not strictly exogenous regressors. We can proceed based on the AR(1) serial correlation test, i.e. simply a t test on $\hat{u}_{t-4}$ for all $t = 5, \ldots, T$. With monthly data, we can test for correlation using a regression of $\hat{u}_t$ on $\hat{u}_{t-12}$.

Next we present an illustrative example using the Phillips data again.

5.2.1 Numerical Example

To determine whether there is a trade-off, on average, between unemployment and inflation, we test $H_0{:}\beta_1 = 0$ against $H_1{:}\beta_1 \neq 0$, where β_1 is the slope in the postulated model. We could use the following fitted equation:

$$\widehat{inf}_t = 1.4236 + 0.4676\, unem_t$$

with $T = 49$, $R^2 = 0.053$, $t = 1.62$ and p value $= 0.11$,
and use the usual OLS t statistic, if the classical linear model assumptions hold.

The fitted equation is obtained in SAS EG by clicking **Tasks** → **Regression** → **Linear Regression** with the results presented in Output 5.1. However, the CLM assumptions do not hold, as we will see below when we conduct our test for serial correlation.

We resume in SAS EG as follows:

1. In the current project, under **Project Tree—Process Flow**, double-click **Linear Regression** to get back to the input data from the results, or simply import the data again.

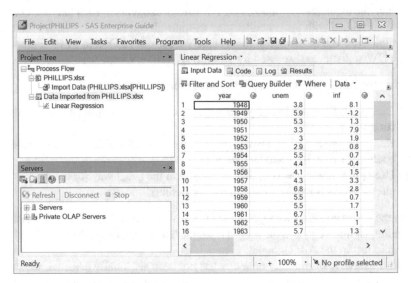

2. Select **Tasks** → **Time Series** → **Regression Analysis with Autoregressive Errors** → **Data** with inf as the dependent variable and $unem$ as the explanatory variable.

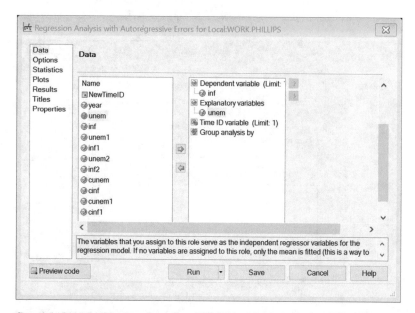

3. In **Options** select **Unconditional least squares estimates**, and then in **Plots**
   select **All appropriate plots for the current data selection**.

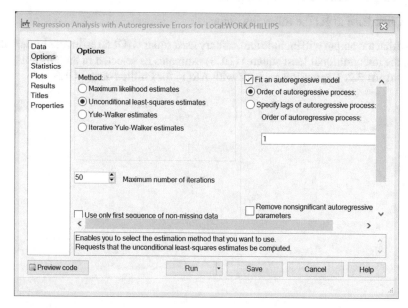

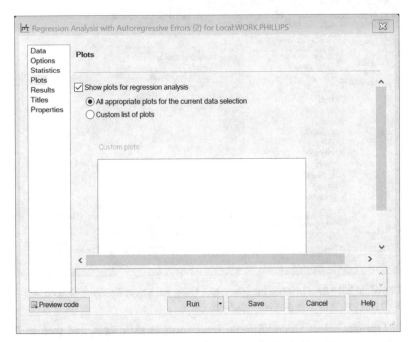

4. Click **Run** to get the following output.

Note that the output will include the ordinary least squares (OLS) estimates by default, and the unconditional least squares (ULS) estimates as selected in the **Options**.

Output 5.2: Regression analysis with AR(1) for Phillips data—OLS

Regression Analysis with Autoregressive Errors
The AUTOREG Procedure

Dependent Variable   inf

Generated by the SAS System ('Local', W32_8PRO) on 28 January 2019 at 11:16:13 AM

Page Break

Regression Analysis with Autoregressive Errors
The AUTOREG Procedure

Ordinary Least Squares Estimates			
SSE	460.619776	DFE	47
MSE	9.80042	Root MSE	3.13056
SBC	256.636495	AIC	252.852855
MAE	2.38412834	AICC	253.113724
MAPE	115.723949	HQC	254.288363
Durbin-Watson	0.8027	Total R-Square	0.0527

Durbin-Watson Statistics	
Order	DW
1	0.8027

Parameter Estimates					
Variable	DF	Estimate	Standard Error	t Value	Approx Pr > |t|
Intercept	1	1.4236	1.7190	0.83	0.4118
unem	1	0.4676	0.2891	1.62	0.1125

Estimates of Autocorrelations			
Lag	Covariance	Correlation	-1 9 8 7 6 5 4 3 2 1 0 1 2 3 4 5 6 7 8 9 1
0	9.4004	1.000000	| |********************|
1	5.3734	0.571616	| |*********** |

Preliminary MSE   6.3289

Estimates of Autoregressive Parameters			
Lag	Coefficient	Standard Error	t Value
1	-0.571616	0.120979	-4.72

Output 5.3: Regression analysis with AR(1) for Phillips data—ULS

Regression Analysis with Autoregressive Errors
The AUTOREG Procedure

Unconditional Least Squares Estimates			
SSE	241.572415	DFE	46
MSE	5.25157	Root MSE	2.29163
SBC	229.881127	AIC	224.205666
MAE	1.50837493	AICC	224.738999
MAPE	75.1205803	HQC	226.358928
Durbin-Watson	1.9673	Transformed Regression R-Square	0.1028
		Total R-Square	0.5032

Durbin-Watson Statistics	
Order	DW
1	1.9673

Parameter Estimates					
Variable	DF	Estimate	Standard Error	t Value	Approx Pr > |t|
Intercept	1	8.3635	2.3960	3.49	0.0011
unem	1	-0.7270	0.3452	-2.11	0.0407
AR1	1	-0.7898	0.0991	-7.97	<.0001

Autoregressive parameters assumed given					
Variable	DF	Estimate	Standard Error	t Value	Approx Pr > |t|
Intercept	1	8.3635	2.2880	3.66	0.0007
unem	1	-0.7270	0.3166	-2.30	0.0263

The above tables report the estimates for the regression parameters and the autoregression parameter ρ, among other statistics.

We have the following fitted equation:

$$\widehat{inf}_t = 8.3635 - 0.7270\, unem_t$$
$$\hat{u}_t = 0.7898\, \hat{u}_{t-1}$$

Note that SAS reports the estimate of ρ with a reversed sign, so $\hat{\rho} = 0.7898$. This is similar to 0.781, the figure reported in Wooldridge (2016, Table 12.2) which is based on a different estimation method. The p value < 0.0001 is smaller than a significance level of 5%, so we have sufficient evidence to conclude the errors are autocorrelated.

Output 5.4: Regression analysis with AR(1) for Phillips data—Diagnostics

Regression Analysis with Autoregressive Errors
The AUTOREG Procedure

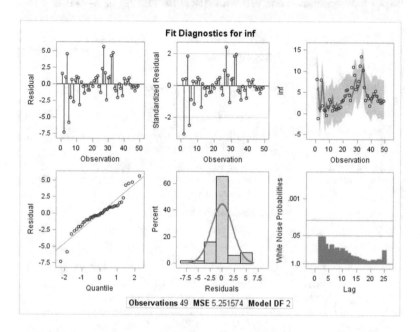

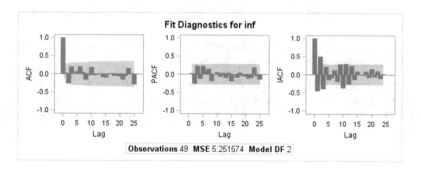

From the residual plots produced, we gather there may exist a few outliers. From the ACF, PACF and IACF plots we do not see strong correlation in the residuals, indicating the model is a satisfactory fit to the data.

Of course, we may select to use the maximum likelihood estimates (MLE) or other alternatives instead of the unconditional least squares estimates. We can do so by clicking **Modify Tasks—Options** to select e.g. maximum likelihood estimates to get the following output.

Output 5.5: Regression analysis with AR(1) for Phillips data—MLE

Regression Analysis with Autoregressive Errors
The AUTOREG Procedure

Maximum Likelihood Estimates			
SSE	241.740564	DFE	46
MSE	5.25523	Root MSE	2.29243
SBC	229.844245	AIC	224.168785
MAE	1.50069103	AICC	224.702118
MAPE	74.8230375	HQC	226.322046
Log Likelihood	-109.08439	Transformed Regression R-Square	0.0970
Durbin-Watson	1.9364	Total R-Square	0.5029
		Observations	49

Durbin-Watson Statistics	
Order	DW
1	1.9364

Parameter Estimates					
Variable	DF	Estimate	Standard Error	t Value	Approx Pr > |t|
Intercept	1	8.2318	2.3553	3.50	0.0011
unem	1	-0.7048	0.3485	-2.02	0.0490
AR1	1	-0.7721	0.1005	-7.68	<.0001

Autoregressive parameters assumed given					
Variable	DF	Estimate	Standard Error	t Value	Approx Pr > |t|
Intercept	1	8.2318	2.2290	3.69	0.0006
unem	1	-0.7048	0.3170	-2.22	0.0312

We see that the tables above contain results slightly different from the OLS and ULS counterparts previously obtained. If the distribution of the data is known to be normally distributed, for example, the MLE would be preferred over OLS and ULS, and vice versa.

Reference

J.M. Wooldridge, *Introductory Econometrics: A Modern Approach*, 6th edn. (Cengage, Boston, 2016)

Chapter 6
Regression Analysis of Panel Data

Abstract In this chapter we will discuss the analysis of panel data. We start with a basic linear regression model, and then focus on both the fixed and random effects models with the required tests for random effects before modelling the suitable data. We also cover the Parks method for the AR(1) error structure. We include numerical examples to illustrate the SAS EG procedure.

Keywords Fixed effects · Hausman test · Panel data · Parks method · Random effects

6.1 Panel Data

Panel data tracks the behaviour of subjects over time. These objects may be individuals, companies or countries. For example, we may be interested in the GDP of certain countries over time. The countries are the subjects and the panel data set is created by tabulating the GDPs of these countries at different points in time.

There are certain advantages to panel data. A basic advantage is the increase in sample size from the collection of data over multiple time periods. Other advantages include its allowance for individual heterogeneity—the ability to control variables that are unobservable, and also flexibility when modelling different behaviours across subjects.

We consider the following framework for modelling panel data:

$$y_{it} = x'_{it}\beta + z'_i\alpha + \lambda_t + u_{it} \tag{6.1}$$

where y_{it} is the response, x_{it} is a vector of k time-varying explanatory variables, β is a vector of k parameters, $z'_i\alpha$ is a time-invariant, cross-sectional unit effect and captures the unobserved heterogeneity of the subjects and may be assumed to contain a constant term, λ_t is a cross-sectionally invariant time effect, and u_{it} is the error

Electronic supplementary material The online version of this chapter (https://doi.org/10.1007/978-981-15-0321-4_6) contains supplementary material, which is available to authorized users.

term of subject i at time t, $i = 1, \ldots, n$ and $t = 1, \ldots, T$, where n is the number of subjects and T is the number of time periods.

To illustrate the computations for the different panel data models, we use the Christenson Associates airline cost data taken from Greene (2012). It was extensively analysed by Ajmani (2009), and by SAS/ETS 15.1 User's Guide (2018), Examples 25.1, 27.3 and 27.4 of the PANEL Procedure (which are available online; their websites are provided in Appendix A.2).

The data contains repeated measurements of costs, outputs, prices of inputs and utilisation rates for six US airlines over the years 1970–1984. The variable C is the total cost (in \$000's), Q is the output in revenue passenger miles (the number of passengers paying revenue times the number of miles flown by the airline in the given time period), FP is the fuel price, and LF is the load factor which measures the percentage of available seating capacity that is filled by passengers.

This data set can be treated as a panel data set with $n = 6$ subjects and $T = 15$ time periods. In this illustration, we analyse the log transformations of the cost ($\ln C$), output quantity ($\ln Q$) and fuel price ($\ln FP$), and the raw load factor (LF).

Firstly, the following basic or pooled model can be fitted as in e.g. Ajmani (2009) and SAS Example 25.1 of the PANEL Procedure:

$$\ln C_{it} = \beta_0 + \beta_1 \ln Q_{it} + \beta_2 \ln FP_{it} + \beta_3 LF_{it} + u_{it} \tag{6.2}$$

where $i = 1, \ldots, 6$ and $t = 1, \ldots, 15$.

The pooled model is the standard ordinary least squares (OLS) regression without any cross-sectional or time effects. The treatment of the heterogeneity effect determines the type of model, so there are several variations of the above model which can be used for panel data. We will mainly discuss two types of models, namely the fixed effects and random effects models. We will also discuss the Parks (1967) autoregressive model as it is available in SAS EG.

6.2   Fixed Effects

The fixed effects model shows the relationship between the response and explanatory variables within a particular subject. Each subject is unique and has its own characteristics which may affect the explanatory variables. When using this model, we assume that bias which can affect the response or explanatory variables exists and hence needs to be controlled. The fixed effects model should be used whenever we are interested in the impact of variables that change over time.

The specific model derived from framework (6.1) above is in the form:

$$y_{it} = x'_{it}\beta + \alpha_i + u_{it}$$

where y_{it} is the response of subject i at time t, x_{it} is a vector of k observed explanatory variables, β is a vector of k parameters, α_i (instead of $z'_i\alpha$ in the framework) can be viewed as the subject-specific intercept terms, and u_{it} is the error term, $i = 1, \ldots, n$ and $t = 1, \ldots, T$.

Note that this representation results in a common vector of parameters β but different intercept terms i.e. the subject-specific constant terms α_i. In the simple linear regression case, this leads to different regression lines for the different subjects where the lines have the same slope but different intercepts (parallel to each other).

Corresponding to the pooled model (6.2), we have the following one-way fixed effects model:

$$\ln C_{it} = \beta_0 + \beta_1 \ln Q_{it} + \beta_2 \ln FP_{it} + \beta_3 LF_{it} + \alpha_i + u_{it} \tag{6.3}$$

where $i = 1, \ldots, 6$ and $t = 1, \ldots, 15$.

6.2.1 Numerical Example

In the first illustrative model, we assume that the individual effects are fixed, and more importantly, common across all subjects (pooled) such that $z'_i\alpha = \alpha_i = \alpha, i = 1, \ldots, n$. The model parameters can therefore be estimated using the ordinary least-squares (OLS) method. SAS EG can be used to fit the regression model (6.2) to the data. The analysis results are given in Output 6.1, same as those produced by the SAS code in Ajmani (2009).

We perform the following steps:

1. Click **File** → **Import Data** to open the data AIRLINE COST.xlsx.

	I	T	lnC	lnQ	lnFP	LF
1	1	1	13.947100…	-0.048395…	11.577307…	0.534487
2	1	2	14.010822…	-0.013331…	11.611022…	0.532328
3	1	3	14.0852094	0.0879925…	11.613440…	0.547736
4	1	4	14.228632…	0.1619317…	11.711563…	0.540846
5	1	5	14.332356…	0.1485665…	12.188957…	0.591167
6	1	6	14.4163999	0.1602122…	12.489780…	0.575417
7	1	7	14.520037…	0.2550374…	12.481622…	0.594495
8	1	8	14.654816…	0.3297856…	12.664797…	0.597409
9	1	9	14.785971…	0.4779283…	12.858684…	0.638522
10	1	10	14.993432…	0.6018210…	13.252076…	0.676287
11	1	11	15.147282…	0.4356968…	13.678127…	0.605735
12	1	12	15.1681835	0.4238942…	13.812745…	0.61436
13	1	13	15.200809…	0.5069380…	13.751507…	0.633366
14	1	14	15.270136…	0.6001049…	13.664189…	0.650117
15	1	15	15.373301…	0.6608615…	13.621210…	0.625603
16	2	1	13.252148…	-0.652706…	11.550173…	0.490851
17	2	2	13.370182…	-0.626185…	11.621573…	0.473449
18	2	3	13.564038…	-0.422826…	11.684051…	0.503013
19	2	4	13.814804…	-0.233730…	11.650920…	0.512501

Data Imported from AIRLINE COST.xlsx ·

Filter and Sort   Query Builder   Where | Data ·

2. Select **Tasks** → **Regression** → **Linear Regression** → **Data** → **Variables to assign** to choose the dependent and explanatory variables as below.

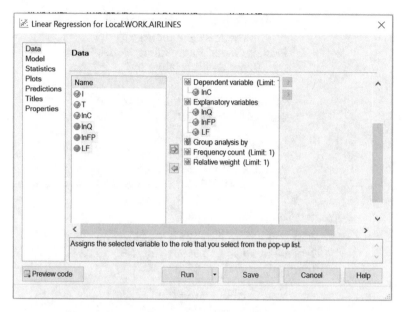

3. Click **Run** to produce the following output.

Output 6.1: The pooled model for the airlines data using OLS

Linear Regression Results

The REG Procedure
Model: Linear_Regression_Model
Dependent Variable: lnC

Number of Observations Read	90
Number of Observations Used	90

Analysis of Variance					
Source	DF	Sum of Squares	Mean Square	F Value	Pr > F
Model	3	112.70545	37.56848	2419.34	<.0001
Error	86	1.33544	0.01553		
Corrected Total	89	114.04089			

Root MSE	0.12461	R-Square	0.9883
Dependent Mean	13.36561	Adj R-Sq	0.9879
Coeff Var	0.93234		

Parameter Estimates					
Variable	DF	Parameter Estimate	Standard Error	t Value	Pr > |t|
Intercept	1	9.51692	0.22924	41.51	<.0001
lnQ	1	0.88274	0.01325	66.60	<.0001
lnFP	1	0.45398	0.02030	22.36	<.0001
LF	1	-1.62751	0.34530	-4.71	<.0001

The fitted model (6.2) is:

$$\ln \hat{C} = 9.5169 + 0.8827 \ln Q + 0.4540 \ln FP - 1.6275 \, LF$$

We see that the sample has 90 observations, the estimate of the variance for the model is $\hat{\sigma}^2 = 0.0155$, the root mean square error is $\hat{\sigma} = 0.1246$, and the coefficient of determination $R^2 = 0.9883$ and the adjusted $R^2 = 0.9879$ are both very high. The coefficients for the explanatory variables are all statistically significant. The signs of the coefficients in the model make intuitive sense—the cost of the airline increases with increases in output quantity and fuel price but decreases with increases in load factor. Because cost, quantity and fuel price are log-transformed, the coefficients for quantity and fuel price are interpreted as elasticities of cost. The coefficient for ln FP is 0.4540, meaning that we would associate a 1% increase in fuel price with a 0.454% increase in cost. For further details, see e.g. Ajmani (2009).

In the second model, which is the one-way fixed effects model (6.3):

$$\ln C_{it} = \beta_0 + \beta_1 \ln Q_{it} + \beta_2 \ln FP_{it} + \beta_3 LF_{it} + \alpha_i + u_{it}$$

we assume that the individual effects are constant but are not common across the subjects, i.e. $\alpha_i \neq \alpha, i = 1, \ldots, n$. Therefore, each α_i needs to be estimated along with β.

The following steps are performed.

1. Import the Airline Cost data as below.

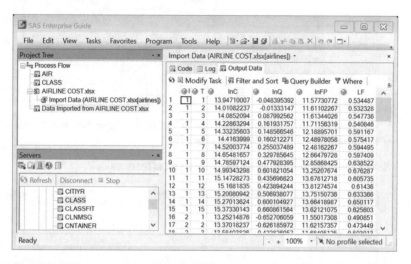

2. Select **Tasks** → **Time Series** → **Regression Analysis of Panel Data** → **Data** → **Variables to assign**.

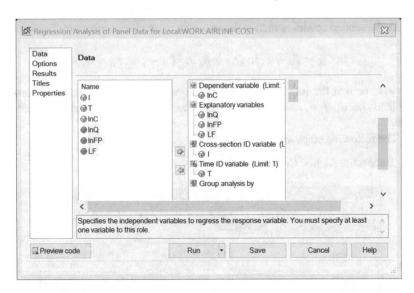

3.   Select **Options** and select a **One-way fixed effects** model.

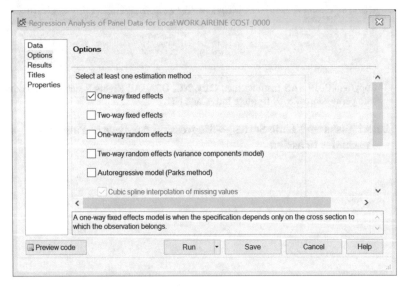

4. Click **Run** to fit the panel model.

Output 6.2: One-way fixed effects model for the airlines data

Regression Analysis of Panel Data
The TSCSREG Procedure
Fixed One-Way Estimates

Dependent Variable: lnC

Model Description	
Estimation Method	FixOne
Number of Cross Sections	6
Time Series Length	15

Fit Statistics			
SSE	0.2926	DFE	81
MSE	0.0036	Root MSE	0.0601
R-Square	0.9974		

F Test for No Fixed Effects			
Num DF	Den DF	F Value	Pr > F
5	81	57.73	<.0001

Parameter Estimates						
Variable	DF	Estimate	Standard Error	t Value	Pr > |t|	Label
CS1	1	-0.08706	0.0842	-1.03	0.3042	Cross Sectional Effect 1
CS2	1	-0.1283	0.0757	-1.69	0.0941	Cross Sectional Effect 2
CS3	1	-0.29598	0.0500	-5.92	<.0001	Cross Sectional Effect 3
CS4	1	0.097494	0.0330	2.95	0.0041	Cross Sectional Effect 4
CS5	1	-0.06301	0.0239	-2.64	0.0100	Cross Sectional Effect 5
Intercept	1	9.793004	0.2637	37.14	<.0001	Intercept
lnQ	1	0.919285	0.0299	30.76	<.0001	
lnFP	1	0.417492	0.0152	27.47	<.0001	
LF	1	-1.0704	0.2017	-5.31	<.0001	

From the description in the output we see that the one-way fixed effects model is fit using the TSCSREG (time series cross section regression) Procedure in SAS which is actually similar to the PANEL procedure, as listed in Appendix A.2. There are 6 cross sections and 15 time observations in the data. As reported, the number of degrees of freedom of the estimate is 81, obtained by the number of observations (90) subtracting the 5 cross section dummy variables and 4 regressors. The Root MSE = 0.0601. The coefficient of determination is very high at $R^2 = 0.9974$, indicating the model is a very good fit to the data.

The F test for no fixed effects provides a F statistic of 57.73 and a very small p value < 0.0001, suggesting the null hypothesis which states that there are no fixed effects is easily rejected. Therefore the test is highly significant, suggesting that there are group effects and the pooled OLS would not give reasonable results as the one-way fixed effects model.

Using such a model to fit the data allows us to obtain the group effects estimates and their standard errors. The estimate for the intercept is the group effects value for the sixth subject $\hat{\alpha}_6 = 9.793$. The estimates for the other group effects are then calculated by adding the variables CS_i to the intercept, e.g. $\hat{\alpha}_1 = \hat{\alpha}_6 + CS_1 = 9.706$. The six group effects estimates are:

$$\hat{\alpha}_1 = 9.706, \ \hat{\alpha}_2 = 9.665, \ \hat{\alpha}_3 = 9.497, \ \hat{\alpha}_4 = 9.890, \ \hat{\alpha}_5 = 9.729, \ \hat{\alpha}_6 = 9.793.$$

The fitted models for the six airlines are given as

Airline 1: $\ln \hat{C} = 9.706 + 0.9192 \ln Q + 0.4174 \ln FP - 1.070 LF$
Airline 2: $\ln \hat{C} = 9.665 + 0.9192 \ln Q + 0.4174 \ln FP - 1.070 LF$
Airline 3: $\ln \hat{C} = 9.497 + 0.9192 \ln Q + 0.4174 \ln FP - 1.070 LF$
Airline 4: $\ln \hat{C} = 9.890 + 0.9192 \ln Q + 0.4174 \ln FP - 1.070 LF$
Airline 5: $\ln \hat{C} = 9.729 + 0.9192 \ln Q + 0.4174 \ln FP - 1.070 LF$
Airline 6: $\ln \hat{C} = 9.793 + 0.9192 \ln Q + 0.4174 \ln FP - 1.070 LF$

Note that only the intercept differs in each of the equations, indicating a parametric shift in the regression lines. Comparing the two models, we see that the signs of the parameter estimates are the same but the magnitude of the coefficient for LF from model (6.3) is significantly lower than that from model (6.2). The Root MSE for model (6.3) is significantly smaller than the counterpart for model (6.2). This is because model (6.3) essentially blocks out the group effects and therefore gives a more precise estimate. The R^2 for model (6.3) is slightly higher than that for model (6.2).

In the third case, we consider a two-way fixed effects model to deal with possible group effects and/or time effects:

$$y_{it} = x'_{it}\beta + \alpha_i + \gamma_t + u_{it}$$

where α_i is the group effect for individual i and γ_t is the time effect at year t.

1. In **Options**, select the **Two-way fixed effects** option.

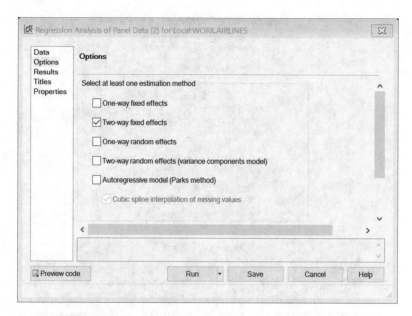

Copyright 2019 SAS Institute Inc., Cary, NC, USA. All Rights Reserved. Reproduced with permission of SAS Institute Inc., Cary, NC

2. Click **Run** to produce the model output.

Output 6.3: Two-way fixed effects model for the airlines data

Regression Analysis of Panel Data
The TSCSREG Procedure
Fixed Two-Way Estimates

Dependent Variable: lnC

Model Description	
Estimation Method	FixTwo
Number of Cross Sections	6
Time Series Length	15

Fit Statistics			
SSE	0.1768	DFE	67
MSE	0.0026	Root MSE	0.0514
R-Square	0.9984		

F Test for No Fixed Effects			
Num DF	Den DF	F Value	Pr > F
19	67	23.10	<.0001

Parameter Estimates							
Variable	DF	Estimate	Standard Error	t Value	Pr > |t|	Label	
CS1	1	0.174282	0.0861	2.02	0.0470	Cross Sectional Effect	1
CS2	1	0.111451	0.0780	1.43	0.1575	Cross Sectional Effect	2
CS3	1	-0.14351	0.0519	-2.77	0.0073	Cross Sectional Effect	3
CS4	1	0.180209	0.0321	5.61	<.0001	Cross Sectional Effect	4
CS5	1	-0.04669	0.0225	-2.08	0.0415	Cross Sectional Effect	5
TS1	1	-0.69314	0.3378	-2.05	0.0441	Time Series Effect	1
TS2	1	-0.63843	0.3321	-1.92	0.0588	Time Series Effect	2
TS3	1	-0.5958	0.3294	-1.81	0.0750	Time Series Effect	3
TS4	1	-0.54215	0.3189	-1.70	0.0938	Time Series Effect	4
TS5	1	-0.47304	0.2319	-2.04	0.0454	Time Series Effect	5
TS6	1	-0.4272	0.1884	-2.27	0.0266	Time Series Effect	6
TS7	1	-0.39598	0.1733	-2.28	0.0255	Time Series Effect	7
TS8	1	-0.33985	0.1501	-2.26	0.0268	Time Series Effect	8
TS9	1	-0.27189	0.1348	-2.02	0.0477	Time Series Effect	9
TS10	1	-0.22739	0.0763	-2.98	0.0040	Time Series Effect	10
TS11	1	-0.1118	0.0319	-3.50	0.0008	Time Series Effect	11
TS12	1	-0.03364	0.0429	-0.78	0.4357	Time Series Effect	12
TS13	1	-0.01773	0.0363	-0.49	0.6263	Time Series Effect	13
TS14	1	-0.01865	0.0305	-0.61	0.5432	Time Series Effect	14
Intercept	1	12.94003	2.2182	5.83	<.0001	Intercept	
lnQ	1	0.817249	0.0319	25.66	<.0001		
lnFP	1	0.168611	0.1635	1.03	0.3061		
LF	1	-0.88281	0.2617	-3.37	0.0012		

We see from the output that the two-way fixed effects model is fitted with the 6 cross sections and 15 time observations. The degrees of freedom of the estimate is 67, obtained from 90 subtracting 5 cross section dummy variables, 14 time dummy variables and 4 regressors. The $R^2 = 0.9984$ is very high and indicates that the model fits very well. The F test for fixed effects tests the null hypothesis which states that there are no fixed effects. We easily reject the null hypothesis as the p value is very small and so we can conclude that there are group effects, or time effects, or both. The OLS would not give reasonable results.

From the parameter estimates, we can see a more complicated pattern. For further analysis, see e.g. Ajmani (2009).

6.3 Random Effects

In the fixed effects analysis, it is assumed that the selected subjects represent the entire population of subjects who are available for the study. On the other hand, if the subjects were selected from a much larger population, then it may have been reasonable to assume that the differences among the subjects were randomly distributed across the population.

A random effects model used for analysing panel data is:

$$y_{it} = x'_{it}\beta + v_i + \lambda_t + u_{it} \tag{6.4}$$

where y_{it} is the response of subject i at time t, v_i is independent and identically distributed (iid) with zero mean and variance σ_v^2, λ_t is iid with zero mean and variance σ_λ^2, u_{it} is iid with zero mean and variance σ_u^2, $i = 1,\ldots,n; t = 1,\ldots,T$. Furthermore, it is assumed that the error terms are mutually uncorrelated and each error term is uncorrelated with x.

The one-way random effects model we consider is a special case of (6.4) i.e. a time-invariant case with $\lambda_t = 0$. The two-way random effects model is as given by (6.4). Both the one-way and two-way random effects models are available in SAS EG. When fitting a random effects model, Hausman's (1978) test can be used to determine whether the fixed effects or the random effects model is more appropriate for the panel data. It tests the null hypothesis of no correlation between the unobserved subject-specific effects and the observed predictor variables versus the alternative hypothesis that the unobserved subject-specific effects are correlated to the observed predictor variables. Rejection of the null hypothesis suggests that the fixed effects model is more appropriate.

In general, random effects models are more efficient than fixed effects models, but tend to not be consistent if the random effects assumption does not hold. For more information on tests for random effects and comparisons between fixed and random effects models with examples, see e.g. Ajmani (2009) and Greene (2012).

6.3.1 Numerical Example

We continue to use the airline cost data to illustrate how our testing and estimation can be done using random effects models. We start with a one-way random effects model.

1. In **Options**, select **One-way random effects** model.

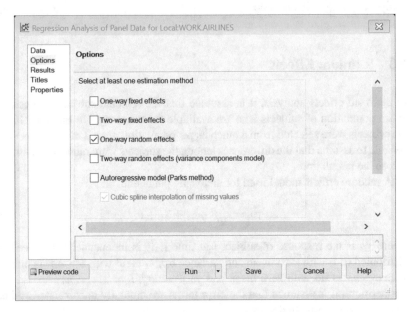

2. Click **Run** to produce the output.

Output 6.4: One-way random effects model assuming random subjects, with the Hausman test for random effects

Regression Analysis of Panel Data
The TSCSREG Procedure
Fuller and Battese Variance Components (RanOne)

Dependent Variable: lnC

Model Description	
Estimation Method	RanOne
Number of Cross Sections	6
Time Series Length	15

Fit Statistics			
SSE	0.3090	DFE	86
MSE	0.0036	Root MSE	0.0599
R-Square	0.9923		

Variance Component Estimates	
Variance Component for Cross Sections	0.018198
Variance Component for Error	0.003613

Hausman Test for Random Effects		
DF	m Value	Pr > m
3	0.92	0.8209

Parameter Estimates					
Variable	DF	Estimate	Standard Error	t Value	Pr > |t|
Intercept	1	9.637	0.2132	45.21	<.0001
lnQ	1	0.908024	0.0260	34.91	<.0001
lnFP	1	0.422199	0.0141	29.95	<.0001
LF	1	-1.06469	0.1995	-5.34	<.0001

The fitted equation is:

$$\ln \hat{C} = 9.6370 + 0.9080 \ln Q + 0.4222 \ln FP - 1.0647 \, LF$$

with $\hat{\sigma}_v^2 = 0.0182$, $\hat{\sigma}_u^2 = 0.0036$, Root MSE $= 0.0599$, $R^2 = 0.9923$ indicating the model fit is very good.

We see from the table above that the p value $= 0.8209$ is not smaller than $\alpha = 0.05$ and so the Hausman test suggests that the individual effects are uncorrelated with the other variables in the model. Hence we would conclude that the random effects model is more appropriate than the fixed effects model for the airlines data.

The individual constant terms in the random effects model are viewed as randomly distributed across cross-sectional units, instead of parametric shifts as in the fixed effects model. This is appropriate when the cross-sectional units are sampled from a large population, and is particularly true in our example where the six airlines are clearly a sample of all the airlines in the industry i.e. the population.

Next, we look at fitting a two-way random effects model.

1. In **Options**, select **Two-way random effects** model.

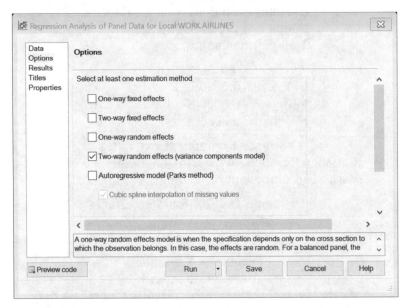

2. Click **Run** to fit the model.

Output 6.5: Two-way random effects model assuming both subjects and time are random, with the Hausman test for random effects

Regression Analysis of Panel Data

The TSCSREG Procedure
Fuller and Battese Variance Components (RanTwo)

Dependent Variable: lnC

Model Description	
Estimation Method	RanTwo
Number of Cross Sections	6
Time Series Length	15

Fit Statistics			
SSE	0.2322	DFE	86
MSE	0.0027	Root MSE	0.0520
R-Square	0.9829		

Variance Component Estimates	
Variance Component for Cross Sections	0.017439
Variance Component for Time Series	0.001081
Variance Component for Error	0.00264

Hausman Test for Random Effects		
DF	m Value	Pr > m
3	6.93	0.0741

Parameter Estimates					
Variable	DF	Estimate	Standard Error	t Value	Pr > |t|
Intercept	1	9.362676	0.2440	38.38	<.0001
lnQ	1	0.866448	0.0255	33.98	<.0001
lnFP	1	0.436163	0.0172	25.41	<.0001
LF	1	-0.98053	0.2235	-4.39	<.0001

The fitted equation is:

$$\ln \hat{C} = 9.3627 + 0.8664 \ln Q + 0.4362 \ln FP - 0.9805\, LF$$

with $\hat{\sigma}_v^2 = 0.0174$, $\hat{\sigma}_\lambda^2 = 0.0011$, $\hat{\sigma}_u^2 = 0.0026$, Root MSE $= 0.0520$ and $R^2 = 0.9829$ indicating the model fit is very good. The Hausman test again suggests that the random effects model is more appropriate than the pooled regression model for the airlines data. This model may be better than the one-way random effects model due to a smaller $\hat{\sigma}_u^2$, or equivalently a smaller Root MSE.

6.4   Parks Method

Parks (1967) considered a model which is included as the last option for Regression Analysis of Panel Data in SAS EG. The model assumed is an AR(1) model with heteroskedasticity and contemporaneous correlation between cross sections. The model and the random errors u_{it} ($i = 1, \ldots, n$ and $t = 1, \ldots, T$) have the following structure:

$$y_{it} = x_{it}\,\beta + u_{it}$$
$$u_{it} = \rho_i\, u_{i,t-1} + \varepsilon_{it}\,\text{(autoregression)}$$

where the required expectations are:

$$E(\varepsilon_{it}) = 0$$
$$E\left(\varepsilon_{it}\,\varepsilon_{jt}\right) = \phi_{ij}$$
$$E\left(\varepsilon_{it}\varepsilon_{js}\right) = 0\,(s \neq t)$$
$$E\left(u_{i,t-1}\varepsilon_{jt}\right) = 0$$
$$E(u_{i0}) = 0$$
$$E\left(u_{i0}u_{j0}\right) = \sigma_{ij} = \phi_{ij}/\left(1 - \rho_i\rho_j\right)$$
$$E\left(u_{it}^2\right) = \sigma_{ii}\,\text{(heteroskedasticity)}$$
$$E\left(u_{it}u_{jt}\right) = \sigma_{ij}\,\text{(contemporaneous correlation)}$$

We see that the random errors are assumed to have an AR(1) structure for each cross section. As a result, the model has n extra first-order autoregressive parameters ρ_i, a correlation matrix for u and a Phi matrix for ε. A consistent estimator of ρ_i, the covariance matrix for the vector of random errors, and an estimated generalised least-squares of β with an estimated Phi matrix involved can be found in SAS/ETS 15.1 User's Guide; for details visit the PANEL Procedure website listed in Appendix A.2.

6.4.1 Numerical Example

Let's continue to use the airline cost data. We can fit an autoregressive model as follows.

1. Click **Options** to select **Autoregressive model (Parks method)** and by defaut **Include the intercept parameter in the model**.

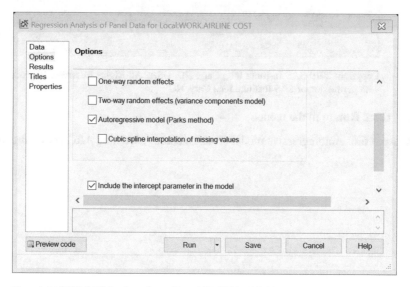

2. Click **Results** to select **Show analysis** with **Correlations of parameter esti-mates, Covariances of parameter estimates, Phi matrix (Parks method only)** and **Autocorrelation coefficients (Parks method only)**.

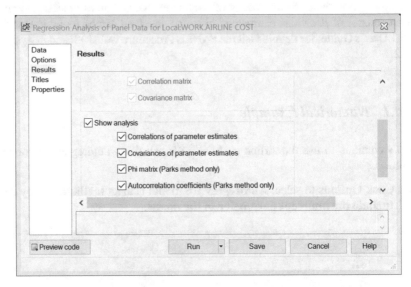

3. Click **Run** to fit the model.

Output 6.6: Autoregressive model (Parks method) assuming AR(1) error structure

Regression Analysis of Panel Data

The TSCSREG Procedure
Parks Method Estimation

Dependent Variable: lnC

Model Description	
Estimation Method	Parks
Number of Cross Sections	6
Time Series Length	15

Fit Statistics			
SSE	62.0510	DFE	86
MSE	0.7215	Root MSE	0.8494
R-Square	0.9941		

Parameter Estimates					
Variable	DF	Estimate	Standard Error	t Value	Pr > |t|
Intercept	1	9.891732	0.1954	50.61	<.0001
lnQ	1	0.887614	0.0117	75.96	<.0001
lnFP	1	0.412129	0.0157	26.28	<.0001
LF	1	-1.34975	0.1553	-8.69	<.0001

Covariances of Parameter Estimates				
	Intercept	lnQ	lnFP	LF
Intercept	0.038194	0.001227	-.002676	-.002413
lnQ	0.001227	0.000137	-.000045	-.000620
lnFP	-.002676	-.000045	0.000246	-.000978
LF	-.002413	-.000620	-.000978	0.024131

Correlations of Parameter Estimates				
	Intercept	lnQ	lnFP	LF
Intercept	1.00000	0.53723	-0.87317	-0.07948
lnQ	0.53723	1.00000	-0.24370	-0.34182
lnFP	-0.87317	-0.24370	1.00000	-0.40138
LF	-0.07948	-0.34182	-0.40138	1.00000

First Order Autoregressive Parameter Estimates	
I	Rho
1	0.919440
2	0.606435
3	0.950887
4	0.971886
5	0.327119
6	0.448636

Estimated Phi Matrix						
	1	2	3	4	5	6
1	0.001374	0.000706	0.000074	-.000329	0.000319	0.000408
2	0.000706	0.004363	0.001652	0.000436	0.001174	0.001801
3	0.000074	0.001652	0.002436	0.000734	0.001677	0.000748
4	-.000329	0.000436	0.000734	0.004962	0.000775	0.001935
5	0.000319	0.001174	0.001677	0.000775	0.002157	0.000926
6	0.000408	0.001801	0.000748	0.001935	0.000926	0.003236

We see that the estimates of the regression parameters β, AR(1) parameters ρ_i and the Phi matrix are reported, among other statistics.

The fitted model is:

$$\ln \hat{C} = 9.8917 + 0.8876 \ln Q + 0.4121 \ln FP - 1.3498 LF$$

with the six AR(1) equations based on $\hat{\rho}_i$

Airline 1: $\hat{u}_{1t} = 0.9194\, \hat{u}_{1,t-1}$
Airline 2: $\hat{u}_{2t} = 0.6064\, \hat{u}_{2,t-1}$
Airline 3: $\hat{u}_{3t} = 0.9509\, \hat{u}_{3,t-1}$
Airline 4: $\hat{u}_{4t} = 0.9719\, \hat{u}_{4,t-1}$
Airline 5: $\hat{u}_{5t} = 0.3271\, \hat{u}_{5,t-1}$
Airline 6: $\hat{u}_{6t} = 0.4486\, \hat{u}_{6,t-1}$

where $\text{Root MSE} = 0.8494$, and where $R^2 = 0.9941$ is very high, indicating the model fit is very good. The t statistics suggest that all the parameters β are significantly different from 0.

In addition, we see that for all six airlines, the errors are positively autocorrelated with differing positive values of $\hat{\rho}_i$ ($i = 1, \ldots, 6$), indicating varying levels of strength. The elements in the estimated Phi matrix reflect the covariances between the errors in the AR(1) equations for the six airlines, which are all positive except for the negative one between airlines 1 and 4.

Note that the AR(1) parameter estimates $\hat{\rho}_i$ and the Phi matrix are only reported by the Parks method, which considers the AR(1) error structure not previously covered by the pooled, fixed effects and random effects models for panel data.

References

V.B. Ajmani, *Applied Econometrics Using the SAS® System* (Wiley, Hoboken, 2009)

W.H. Greene, *Econometric Analysis*, 7th edn. (Pearson, London, 2012)

J.A. Hausman, Specification tests in econometrics. Econometrica **46**, 1251–1271 (1978)

R.W. Parks, Efficient estimation of a system of regression equations when disturbances are both serially and contemporaneously correlated. J. Am. Stat. Assoc. **62**, 500–509 (1967)

Appendix

A.1 List of Data Sets Used in the Book

Air data, or Airline Passenger data, Box and Jenkins (1976); also available in the SASHELP library
Airline data, or Airline Cost data, Greene (2012)
Class data, available in the SASHELP library
Phillips data, Wooldridge (2016)
Retail Turnover data, Australian Bureau of Statistics, Cat. No. 8501.0; also Berenson et al. (2013)
Steel data, available in the SASHELP library
Unemployed Persons data, Australian Bureau of Statistics, Cat. No. 6291.0.55.003; also Berenson et al. (2013)
Vegemite Price data, Berenson et al. (2013).

A.2 List of SAS Online Examples

The ARIMA Procedure

Example 7.2 Seasonal Model for the Airline Series
http://documentation.sas.com/?docsetId=etsug&docsetTarget=etsug_arima_examples02.htm&docsetVersion=15.1&locale=en

The AUTOREG Procedure

Example 8.1 Analysis of Real Output Series
http://documentation.sas.com/?docsetId=etsug&docsetTarget=etsug_autoreg_examples01.htm&docsetVersion=15.1&locale=en

The PANEL Procedure

Example 25.1 The Airline Cost Data: Fixed Effects
http://documentation.sas.com/?docsetId=etsug&docsetTarget=etsug_panel_
examples01.htm&docsetVersion=15.1&locale=en

The PANEL Procedure

Example 27.3 The Airline Cost Data: Further Analysis
http://support.sas.com/documentation/cdl/en/etsug/68148/HTML/default/viewer.
htm#etsug_panel_examples04.htm

The PANEL Procedure

Example 27.4 The Airline Cost Data: Random-Effects Models
http://support.sas.com/documentation/cdl/en/etsug/68148/HTML/default/viewer.
htm#etsug_panel_examples05.htm

The PANEL Procedure

Parks Method for Autoregressive Models (PARKS Option)
https://documentation.sas.com/?docsetId=etsug&docsetTarget=etsug_panel_
details23.htm&docsetVersion=15.1&locale=en

The REG Procedure

Simple Linear Regression
https://documentation.sas.com/?docsetId=statug&docsetTarget=statug_reg_
gettingstarted01.htm&docsetVersion=15.1&locale=en

References

M.L. Berenson, D.M. Levine, T.C. Krehbiel, D.F. Stephan, M.O'Brien, N. Jayne, J. Watson, *Basic Business Statistics: Concepts and Applications,* 3rd edn. (Pearson, London, 2013)

G.E.P. Box, G.M. Jenkins, *Time Series Analysis: Forecasting and Control.* Revised edn. (Holden-Day, San Francisco, 1976)

W.H. Greene, *Econometric Analysis*, 7th edn. (Pearson, London, 2012)

J.M. Wooldridge, *Introductory Econometrics: A Modern Approach*. 6th edn. (Cengage, Boston, 2016)

Glossary

Alternative Hypothesis The hypothesis against which the null hypothesis is tested.

AR(1) Model [Autoregressive Model of Order One] A time series model whose current value depends linearly on its most recent value plus an unpredictable disturbance.

Autocorrelation [Serial Correlation] Correlation between data values in consecutive periods of time in a time series or panel data model.

Augmented Dickey-Fuller Test A test for stationarity that includes lagged changes of the variable as regressors.

Autoregressive Moving Average (ARMA) Model A tool for understanding or predicting future values for a time series. The AR part involves regressing the variable on its own past values. The MA part involves modelling the error term as a linear combination of error terms occurring contemporaneously and at various times in the past.

Correlation Coefficient A measure of the relative strength of the linear relationship between two numerical variables and is bounded between -1 and 1, inclusive.

Covariance A measure of the strength of the linear relationship between two numerical variables.

Covariance Stationary A time series with constant mean and variance where the covariance between any two numerical variables in the sequence depends only on the distance between them.

Cross Sectional Data Data collected by sampling a population at a given point in time.

Dependent Variable The variable that is explained in a regression model.

Descriptive Statistic A statistic used to summarise a set of numbers, e.g. the sample mean, median or standard deviation.

Dickey-Fuller (DF) Test A test for stationarity in an AR(1) model.

Durbin-Watson Test A test for AR(1) serial correlation in the errors of a time series regression model under the classical linear model assumptions.

Exogenous Explanatory Variable An explanatory variable that is uncorrelated with the error term.

© The Author(s), under exclusive license to Springer Nature Singapore Pte Ltd. 2020   127
T. Liu et al., *Time Series Analysis Using SAS Enterprise Guide*, SpringerBriefs
in Statistics, https://doi.org/10.1007/978-981-15-0321-4

Explanatory [Independent] Variable A variable that is used to explain variation in the dependent variable in a regression model.

Exponential Smoothing A simple method of forecasting a variable that involves a weighting of all previous outcomes on that variable.

Fixed Effects Model A model for panel data where longitudinal observations exist for the same subject, with the subject-specific effects being fixed (non-random) or allowed to be associated with the explanatory variables.

Heteroskedasticity The variance of the error term is not constant given the explanatory variables.

Histogram Graphical representation of a frequency or relative frequency distribution the area of each rectangle represents the class frequency or relative frequency.

Homoskedasticity The errors in a regression model have constant variance conditional on the explanatory variables.

Hypothesis Test A statistical test of the null hypothesis against an alternative hypothesis.

Independent [Explanatory] Variable A variable that is used to explain variation in the dependent variable in a regression model.

Kolmogorov-Smirnov Test A nonparametric test of the equality of probability distributions that can be used to compare a sample with a Normal or another reference distribution, or to compare two samples.

Least Squares Estimator An estimator which minimises the sum of squared residuals.

Line Plot Graphical representation of the value of a numerical variable over time.

MA(1) Model [Moving Average Model of Order One] A time series model generated as a linear function of the current value and one lagged value of a zero mean, constant variance, uncorrelated random errors.

Maximum Likelihood Estimator An estimator that maximises the likelihood function.

Mean Square Error (MSE) The sum of squares due to random error divided by the appropriate degrees of freedom.

Multiple Linear Regression Model A model that uses more than one explanatory variable to explain the variation in the dependent variable.

One-Step-Ahead Forecast A time series forecast one period into the future.

p **Value** Probability of getting a test statistic more extreme than the sample result if the null hypothesis is true.

Panel Data Data constructed from repeated cross sections over time.

Parks Method A procedure that accommodates the autoregressive structure by estimating an AR(1) model with contemporaneous correlation.

R-Square The proportion of variation in the dependent variable that is explained by the explanatory variables.

Random Effects Model A panel data model in which the subject-specific effect is a random variable assumed to be uncorrelated with the explanatory variables in each time period.

Random Error Error that results from unpredictable variations.

Residual The difference between the observed value and the fitted (or predicted) value produced by the regression model.

SAS Enterprise Guide A point-and-click, menu-and-wizard-driven tool that empowers users to analyse data and publish their results.

SAS Procedure A set of SAS codes used to analyse or process a SAS data set to produce statistics, tables, reports, charts, and plots, to create SQL queries, to perform other analyses, and to manage and print SAS files.

SASHELP A SAS library that is made available at the start of a session, with information about the session, views, tables and data sets.

Scatter Plot Graphical representation of the relationship between two numerical variables.

Seasonal Effect The regular seasonal change in a time series.

Seasonal Dummy Variables A set of dummy variables used to denote the quarters or months of the year.

Seasonally Adjusted Monthly or quarterly time series data where some statistical procedure—possibly regression on seasonal dummy variables—has been used to remove the seasonal component.

Serial Correlation [Autocorrelation] Correlation between data values in consecutive periods of time in a time series or panel data model.

Shapiro-Wilk Test A test for normality in Statistics to test whether a sample comes from a Normal distribution.

Simple Linear Regression Model A model that uses a single explanatory variable to predict the dependent variable.

Standard Deviation A measure of variation based on squared deviations from the mean directly related to the variance.

Standard Error The square root of the expected squared difference between the random variable and its expected value.

Static Model A time series model where only contemporaneous explanatory variables affect the dependent variable.

Stationary Series A time series for which the marginal and all joint distributions are invariant across time.

Strictly Exogenous The explanatory variables that are uncorrelated with the error term in all time periods in a time series or panel data model.

***t*Test for the Slope** The hypothesis test for the statistical significance of the regression slope parameter using a t distribution.

Test Statistic A value derived from sample data that is used to determine whether the null hypothesis should be rejected or not.

Time Series Data Data collected at successive points in time on one or more variables.

Trend An overall long-term upward or downward movement in the values of a time series.

Trend-Stationary Series A series that is stationary once the time trend has been removed.

Variance A measure of variation based on squared deviations from the mean directly related to standard deviation.

Variation The amount of scattering of values away from a central value.

z-Score The number of standard deviations a given value is from the mean.

Bibliography

Australian Bureau of Statistics, Cat. No. 6291.0.55.003, Labour Force, Australia, Detailed

Australian Bureau of Statistics, Cat. No. 8501.0, Retail Trade Trends, Australia

Copyright 2018. SAS Institute Inc., *Sashelp Data Sets* (SAS Institute Inc., Cary, NC, USA, 2018). All Rights Reserved

Copyright 2018. SAS Institute Inc., *SAS/ETS® 15.1 User's Guide* (SAS Institute Inc., Cary, NC, USA, 2018). All Rights Reserved. https://support.sas.com/documentation/onlinedoc/ets/151/etshpug.pdf. Last accessed 23 Feb 2019

Copyright 2019. SAS Institute Inc., *SAS Enterprise Guide* (SAS Institute Inc., Cary, NC, USA, 2019). All Rights Reserved. https://support.sas.com/en/software/enterprise-guide-support.html. Last accessed 17 Nov 2019

Copyright 2019. SAS Institute Inc., *Getting Started with SAS Enterprise Guide* (SAS Institute Inc., Cary, NC, USA, 2019). All Rights Reserved. http://support.sas.com/documentation/onlinedoc/guide/tut71/en/menu.htm. Last accessed 16 Feb 2019

United States. President and Council of Economic Advisers (U.S.), 2004 *Economic Report of the President* (U.S. Government Printing Office). https://www.govinfo.gov/app/details/ERP-2004. Last accessed on 15 Nov 2019

© The Author(s), under exclusive license to Springer Nature Singapore Pte Ltd. 2020
T. Liu et al., *Time Series Analysis Using SAS Enterprise Guide*, SpringerBriefs
in Statistics, https://doi.org/10.1007/978-981-15-0321-4